D1446372

THE ACCIDENTAL CHEF

LESSONS LEARNED
IN AND OUT OF THE KITCHEN

A Memoir

CAROLINE ISHII

I have tried to recreate dates, events, locales and conversations from my memories of them. In order to maintain anonymity, in some instances I have changed the names of individuals and places. Where I felt it necessary, I've also changed identifying characteristics and details, such as occupations and places of residence.

Cover design and book design direction: Timothy Jones—tjones@bsl.com

Book layout: Cäcilia Winand

Editing by Laura McGavin—www.crafteditingandwriting.com

Proofreading by Chris Childs

Author cover photograph by Paul Jones

Photo credits:
Photographs courtesy of Mountain Road Productions: pages 18, 138, 154, 158
Page 14: Qi Zhai
Page 70: Krishna Mercer
Page 76: International Federation of Red Cross and Red Crescent Societies
Pages 88, 98, 108: Yuki Itoh
Page 132: Michelle Tribe
Page 144: Jill Pyle
Page 168: Japanese Canadian Cultural Centre
Page 188: Corinna Horton
All other photos were taken by the author or her family.

ISBN 978-1522791812

PRAISE FOR CAROLINE ISHII AND THE ACCIDENTAL CHEF

"Part memoir, part cookbook, *The Accidental Chef* is a beautifully crafted chronicle of Chef Caroline Ishii's life journey from rebellious Japanese-Canadian schoolgirl to celebrated vegan chef. Each chapter relates a pivotal moment in that voyage and ends with a recipe — a 'taste memory' that serves as a touchstone Ishii identifies with a key mentor or major event from her past. In one chapter the author focuses on *kokoro,* a Japanese word used to describe something that comes from the heart. *The Accidental Chef* embodies kokoro—a generous guide and recipe journal offered with love."

Sarah Brown, Former Editor, *Ottawa Magazine*

"Caroline's life story confirms what you instinctively knew if you'd eaten her delicious and innovative vegan dishes—she's a positive, principled, thoughtful person who gives the best of herself for those around her, be they family, friends or customers. This is an uplifting read—and one you'll event want to cook from."

Peter Hum, Food Editor, *Ottawa Citizen*

"Award-winning chef Caroline Ishii is well known for her mastery of exquisite vegan cuisine. In *The Accidental Chef* she serves up a *table d'hôte* of stories from her life, paired with a tantalizing selection of (mostly) vegan recipes. Ishii's style is fresh, insightful, and always genuine...The vegan-curious will learn how to create, in their own kitchens, some of Ishii's favourite dishes and desserts. Japanese-Canadians will relate to the comfort of *ochazuke* ('A Bowl of Rice in the Middle of the Night'). And all readers will be nourished, replenished, and motivated to boldly seek out the true flavours of their lives."

Sachiko Okuda, president, *Ottawa Japanese Community Association,* and Council Member, *National Association of Japanese Canadians*

"I love the way Caroline shares deep, personal stories with a quick flit of words and, boom, there's a lesson and a path. I will be trying Caroline's recipes for exactly the reasons she writes about them: to share with my family, to make and eat them together."

Chef Brad Long, Chef-Owner, Café Belong at Evergreen Brick Works, and co-host of the Food Network's *Restaurant Makeover*

"A heartfelt, helpful and healing book. Highly recommended!"

Jeff Brown, author of *Soulshaping* and *An Uncommon Bond*

To my mother Suyeko and my father George.

Through writing this book, I came to truly understand and appreciate
how much they loved and gave to me.

We write to taste life twice...

— Anaïs Nin, *In Favor of the Sensitive Man*

CONTENTS

PREFACE

I wrote this book to encourage people to follow their dreams and show them that there is magic in using your creative talents, even ones that you didn't know existed. Sometimes talents are hidden well beneath the surface of our fears and obstacles, so the only way to discover them is trying as many things as possible and using your instincts. How do you know if you could be a great musician, artist or dancer if you've never tried? How did I know that I could become an award-winning chef and creator of food that people love? It was on the way to creating my restaurant, ZenKitchen, that I accidently became a chef. The rest, as they say, is history.

I love the movie *The Accidental Tourist,* and my favourite line is when William Hurt says, "Maybe it's not just how much you love someone; maybe what matters is who you are when you are with them." When I was creating ZenKitchen, there were many people who supported me, believed in me, and made me feel the project was possible. They made all the difference. I'm so grateful to the customers and to my family and friends, who knew that I would write this book even before I knew. That's what good people bring to your life: they believe in you and encourage you to get up when you falter in doubt.

Until I started writing, I never realized what profound influences my mother, dad, aunts and uncles had on me, and in particular on why and how I cook. Their influences started from the time I was born, perhaps even before I was born, into a family that has a deep love for eating and sharing food. I have incredible appreciation and gratitude for my family's experiences and stories, which impact the taste memories and recipes I share here.

I always had great admiration for many of the cooks who came through ZenKitchen. They were young and bright. They worked hard at what they did and were proud of their labour. They chose cooking for a reason, and it wasn't for the money—you could have much better pay and conditions in other fields. If they landed in my kitchen, they had a passion for both cooking and learning, because cooking vegan food, in the Zen way, was new to all of them. These cooks had life coursing through their veins. They were *awake* (even though this sometimes took the help of swigging Red Bull!).

By the time I became an accidental chef, I had worked in many office settings that were disturbing. I'd have to check my coworkers' pulses to find out if they were still breathing. They were dying of boredom from having to sit through long, unproductive meetings, or were stressed and anxious from having too much to do in a short time period. It was soul destroying. I wrote this book for you, in the hopes of waking you up through what I do best: nourishing and inspiring others with food and food for thought. I encourage you to follow your dreams, trust your instincts and discover your talents. The world is waiting for you.

THE ACCIDENTAL CHEF

INTRODUCTION

People often ask me how I created ZenKitchen. What was the recipe and why was it so successful? What was the magic ingredient?

ZenKitchen was one of the first vegan fine dining restaurants in Canada. It opened during June 2009 in Ottawa's Chinatown. From its beginnings, Zen-Kitchen was an inclusive, progressive and community-minded project. I had begun holding monthly vegan pop-up dinners two years before the restaurant opened, testing out the concept and food, and I garnered a following from devoted diners, mostly omnivores, who asked me to open a restaurant. In fact, they said they would help me open a restaurant in whatever way they could. I came up with what I called a community-supported restaurant initiative to gather funds in advance from my diners, like a farmer does with community-supported agriculture, or CSA. This fit with my idea that the restaurant would be a collective experience.

I wanted ZenKitchen and my cooking to be as sustainable as possible. I used the usual "green" practices, like recycling, composting and deciding not to sell bottled water. But I also decided that the food would be vegan, without any animal or fish products, including meat, fish, cheese, eggs, milk or even honey. My dishes would be made from scratch with whole, local, organic foods. There would be no preservatives, additives or GMOs in the food, because I knew from my chef training in New York and my own research that chemically treated foods create havoc with our health and the health of our children. I felt responsible to put the most healthful food into my customers' bodies.

Folks caught on quickly. Soon after the restaurant opened its doors, we won a Best New Restaurant of the Year Award from the Ottawa Restaurant Hotel & Motel Association that recognized our impact on the industry. ZenKitchen was often mentioned in lists of top restaurants in the city, and we were named one of the best restaurants in Ontario by *Lonely Planet Canada,* who created a "day-in-the-life" one-pager for their Ottawa section. The frosting on the cake—vegan cake, of course—was when I was asked by Canada's Gold Medal Plates Committee to compete in that prestigious competition with ten of the city's top chefs. I was the first woman in Ottawa, and the first vegan chef in Canada, ever invited to the competition.

But I never promoted ZenKitchen as vegan. When I started the restaurant, most people in Ottawa didn't know what vegan food is, or even how to pronounce the word (it's not "vay-gan"!). Many thought that being vegan had to do with a cult, or with being a hippie, or that vegan food is brown and mushy, not pretty or tasty. I have to admit that sometimes this was the case. I didn't want these negative connotations to be associated with my food before customers even tried the dishes; I wanted diners to eat before making a judgment. I was going to give plant-based food a makeover, and it would be attractive and sexy!

Even though I'm known as a vegan chef, you'll notice I've included a meat dish in this book that honours my food history: my mother's delicious spare ribs. My approach has always been that good food is good food, whether meat, fish, or vegetable. All food needs to be treated with respect and care in the cooking. I am not a vegan, but I am inspired by vegan cuisine because I strongly believe that we need to eat more plant-based foods for the health of our planet and ourselves. And I love how my food at ZenKitchen was inclusive: it brought people together, satisfying most diners. I didn't realize when I first started the restaurant that it would be such a project of inclusivity. Many groups who came in had one or several people who were vegetarian or vegan or who had a dietary restriction, and they could all happily eat the food. ZenKitchen brought a thoughtful and kinder approach, one of thinking about everyone at the table. I still can't understand why we have so many narrow assumptions over the food that people choose to eat. At street stalls in Asia, I've had some amazing food, sometimes vegetarian, sometimes meat or fish, and sometimes a combination of all of the above. The goal of that much-loved street food isn't to highlight a certain protein, but to make and eat the freshest, tastiest dish, whatever it may be. I loved it when *Ottawa Citizen* food critic Anne DesBrisay "got" my food in an article that described "the next decade's trendsetters." "That Caroline Ishii's new restaurant serves exclusively vegan food is largely forgotten as you work your way through dinner at ZenKitchen," she wrote. "And that's what makes this new restaurant extraordinary."

I hope you'll find the recipes in this book extraordinary, too. They capture pivotal moments I experienced in becoming "the accidental chef," a woman who slowly stumbled on a career in food and community by listening to cues and paying attention within. Food has been and continues to be the undercurrent that pushes me forward in my life. To me, food is much more than what we eat. It is love. It is comfort. It has specific meanings and memories for each of us. Each chapter here relates to a taste memory from my life that has special meaning to me, with a recipe that reminds me of people and events throughout my journey to opening ZenKitchen and becoming a professional chef.

Each recipe collected here honours my philosophy for cooking. The food must be beautiful, because we eat first with our eyes. It must also be delicious. I like for food to surprise, because this appeals to the children within us all. Of course, food should be nutritious. Above all, food should always be made with love. Love is the ingredient that feeds our souls.

In fact, this is a book about love: not love of the gushy, romantic kind, but love that starts with caring about food and about others. I put those kinds of love together to start ZenKitchen when I took the first steps towards its creation in 2007. What transpired and its impact on the local food community was beyond my wildest imagination. Creating a restaurant took courage, willingness to look for and listen to the truth, and the ability to know my heart. Reflecting on my life as a chef, I realize that there wasn't much "accidental" about it: even though I didn't plan to be a restaurateur, I got there by honouring my values and abilities, one step at a time.

ZENKITCHEN

As long as I can remember, I wanted to work in a restaurant. This must have been a love affair that my mom passed on, because she loved going out to eat. I also grew up in Toronto, where there are so many delicious food options. My high school friends and I loved to eat various ethnic foods at restaurants throughout the city. By the time I was sixteen, I really wanted to be a server, but I had no experience and was too young. I saw an advertisement at my high school for a community college course in restaurant serving and signed up, lying about my age.

After the course, there were interviews for serving positions at the CN Tower 360 Restaurant. I got an interview and was the only one hired from my class. I was thrilled. I started with the brunch/lunch shift, and moved up to be a team captain. I had to work in a team system because the restaurant was so big, around 400 seats. The real challenge was that the centre of the restaurant, the kitchen, stayed put, while the dining room around it turned continuously as the CN Tower rotated. The turn was set faster on a busy day, because most diners wouldn't leave until they'd completed a full rotation. To save time, we would pick up large trays with eight to twelve lidded plates, which was back-breaking work if you went the wrong way and had to go the long route to your section. I loved serving there, and stayed for several years, full time in the summers and part time during the school year.

Those beginnings were my launch into the restaurant industry. From there, I served on and off for the next ten years in restaurants, bars, and hotels in Toronto and then Ottawa. Despite experiencing the craziness of the business, I still wanted to run a restaurant. My mother had other plans; she wanted me to go to the University of Toronto and become a doctor or lawyer. When I said I didn't want to do this, never mind that my grades would never be high enough, she thought the next best thing would be to fix me up with the high-achieving sons of Japanese friends. I'd come home some days and she would have a big smile and be so sweet opening the door, which was strange because there was usually a lot of friction between us. Then she'd say, "Kaya-chan, come have something to eat." She knew that I loved food and couldn't resist. Next came, "Kaya-chan, I want you to meet..."

Looking back, I was pretty mean to my mom and her chosen prey. I would look at her in disgust, roll my eyes at the shy boy in the corner with the horn-rimmed glasses and nervous smile, and take off to my room quickly, shutting the door. I knew I would hear about it later from Mom, but I didn't care. I had a boyfriend who was *hakujin,* I was working full time serving to make money for college, and I knew I wanted to travel, to leave my mother and our tensions. I had a plan.

The dream of owning a restaurant continued throughout my time as a server, although working as a cook never crossed my mind. I encountered chefs who were hot headed, egotistical, and verbally and physically abusive. One chased me around the kitchen, trying to goose me with a spatula. I knew cooks worked long hours in hot, crowded spaces, which wasn't appealing at all, on top of which they weren't paid much, and I needed to make money for my plan of escape. While I cooked delicious dinners and was the perfect hostess when I had company, for the most part I survived on food that I was given at the restaurant where I worked. I would seldom buy meals because of the expense, and I cooked absolutely basic food for myself.

However, in those early days, I did ask the cooks a lot of questions about how to make this or that. I wanted to explain the food well to customers, but this was also for self-interest. I'd ask during "slow" periods, when I thought the cooks weren't doing anything. Now I realize they were preparing for service, or getting ready to set up or tear down; if they weren't, it was because the chef wasn't around to oversee them. I did help with some prep when I could, but in hindsight, I was probably allowed to linger because I was young, cute, and a nice distraction. Yet these experiences influenced how I would run Zen-Kitchen, and I still use the tips I received.

After some time, my restaurant concept focused. I wanted a place that would resonate with Zen philosophy, having a holistic and mindful approach to cooking, eating, and serving customers. I imagined that it would be simple and bring community together. I collected pictures, sayings, and articles related to Zen and to the café I envisioned. During a Julia Cameron workshop at the Kripalu Center for Yoga & Health in 2004, participants spoke about their dreams, and I mentioned the Zen café shyly, saying that this was only a vision. My group was supportive, and the seed was set in fertile ground. From Julia Cameron, I learned to journal upon waking up in the morning, and to take myself for intentional, creative dates. Thoughts and words meandered through my writing, and I consciously tried on different ideas. The restaurant path seemed to reach out for me like one child does to another, beckoning to come and play for a while. I started to imagine becoming a chef.

Eventually, I took those yearnings and ideas seriously, and made the commitment to train. I completed rigorous chef school in the US, with a focus on vegan and vegetarian cuisine, and I interned at influential restaurants like Candle 79 in New York. But arriving back in Ottawa during early 2007, I didn't know what to do with my new knowledge. I took pause and entertained various options. Would I cater? Teach? Become a personal chef? The name for a restaurant lingered in my mind. I knew I wanted Zen in it. "Café" didn't seem to fit my business ideas, but when I added "kitchen," it worked. The kitchen is the heart of the house, and the food I wanted to create was from the heart, delicious, and comforting.

When I was in New York, dinners held by chefs in their homes and supper clubs were popping up everywhere, before the word "pop-up" was even on the scene. I loved the concept and wanted to try a pop-up in Ottawa, modeled on weekly gourmet dinners by soon-to-be chef graduates or guest chefs at my school. I knew the idea would work. Friends were supportive, as friends can only be, but most people I told thought I was speaking another language. They were skeptical when I talked about vegan cuisine, whole foods, GMOs, or even the idea of cooking with organic, local produce. These ideas were fairly new, except to a handful of diehard chefs who had been making food this way for a long time in Ottawa and other cities in Canada. Some stayed under the radar in case the public thought they were too granola, cultish, or strange.

I knew that cooking and eating this way had been popular in New York City and San Francisco for a long time, not only with vegans and vegetarians, but also with anyone health conscious. People there got it. The first wave of local, organic food came to larger cities in the US during the 1970s, around the time that Greenmarket farmers' markets were created by chefs and farmers to provide fresh produce from local suppliers. The first Greenmarket was launched in Union Square, Manhattan in 1976, and took off to the point that it seems to have always been part of the city. That feeling of necessity and belonging is a sign of something people have been thirsty for. The community comes to drink, not knowing it needed this very thing. I wanted the arrival of ZenKitchen in Ottawa to feel like that.

By 2007, I had the name of my restaurant and I was passionate about making my pop-up concept happen. I don't know where my drive came from, but it kept pushing me forward. I had to find a location. The modest townhouse I shared with my partner, Dave, didn't have space for it. I knew it had to be in a café or restaurant where we could set up and serve a good number of people. I didn't know any chefs or owners who would lend me their space, but I did see that many places were closed a night a week.

And so I started my search like a door-to-door salesperson, calling on places that fit my criteria. Most owners were friendly enough, but I was a chef with no experience, no reputation, and I was going to cook this strange type of cuisine with no meat or fish. They were curious enough to listen to my pitch, but at the end of the day, there was no room at the inn.

One day during my search, I walked into the Roasted Cherry, a downtown coffeehouse that served light food and soup. Its mandate was to help students and the underprivileged gain work experience in a café setting. I had a conversation with the manager while he served my coffee. He was friendly, and perhaps bored, so our chat continued. I decided to make my pitch for having a pop-up dinner there. He listened to what I had to say, loved my concept, and said yes. I did a double take and asked him the question again: "So I can have my dinner here?" He said yes again. I had found my location.

From that point, things rolled out quickly. I set a date for the first dinner, April 13, 2007, and made the arrangements. It was to be a four-course, gourmet vegan dinner and we planned to obtain a special permit to serve wine with the meal. We estimated that we could fit thirty-six people in long communal tables that I would rent. The owner said I could get his staff to serve.

Who to invite? I knew that it would be important to create a special list for the first dinner, made up of friends and contacts that would give us honest feedback and would help spread the word if they liked what they experienced. I started to contact the guest list, explaining the concept and inviting them to be our guest for the evening. Most guests were willing to pay in advance, helping us to offset the costs, even though they didn't know the menu. They showed a healthy mix of curiosity and skepticism about what they would be eating.

I started to create the menu, but I knew that, in order to cook the dinner for this many people, I would need help. My friend Gregg from chef school was now transplanted from New York City to Toronto, and I reached out to him. He was enthusiastic about helping, but also nervous. I had no doubt that we could pull it off, and I suppose my enthusiasm got him involved. Sometimes naiveté and enthusiasm can take you a long way.

The first monthly dinner was a hit and diners were eager for others. At a networking event, I met a woman who had heard about my dinners and was enthusiastic for me to hold one at the place she managed, the Helsinki Lounge in Ottawa's ByWard Market. The second dinner happened there on May 28, 2007. That's the way things went in those days: there was such a great energy around the concept that it attracted supportive people and circumstances at every turn.

For the next dinner, a client said that I should try The Chelsea Club, a historic private club downtown that was created by members of the Women's Canadian Club. The client said she didn't think that the Club had that much on and the chef was very nice. I set up a meeting with Chef Sean Murphy, bringing nothing but my unwavering enthusiasm for the pop-up concept. He confidently told me I'd be welcome to host the dinners there and asked if I would be interested in helping him in the kitchen. I said yes immediately. I believe we could each tell that the other person was a good fit, and it was the start of great friendship. From that point on ZenKitchen was no longer homeless.

The dinners flowed organically during the two years 2007-2009, when we held them at The Chelsea Club. I have some lovely memories of the monthly dinners. There was a special theme for each dinner, with the menu created to support this theme. We sometimes focused on a regional cuisine, like Japanese or Italian, or hosted a wine pairing. We held an Oktoberfest beer pairing with a local craft brewery, had harvest dinners promoting local farms, served comfort food for the winter, and did laughter yoga before diners ate.

In the fall of 2008, I received a few emails announcing that Mountain Road Productions was casting a woman or couple opening a restaurant for a documentary-reality TV show. On the deadline date, October 20, 2008, I showed the messages to my partner Dave. By this time, we were working together on the pop-up dinners and still thought periodically about opening our own location for ZenKitchen. Dave and I figured applying for the show would be a long shot, but we agreed to put in a quick submission. We soon got a call from Mountain Road to meet.

They were looking at several candidates. We got along well with Tim Alp, the president and executive producer, and told his team our story about the monthly dinners. Telling the story, I was doubtful I'd ever open a restaurant, let alone be cast on TV.

They seemed enthusiastic about us and wanted to film a pilot for the W Network. I nodded, not having a clue what I was getting myself into.

The pilot filming date was set for November 11, 2008. After waiting, often outside for a long time and without any of those nice dressing rooms or catering trucks, I had to appear full of energy. I kept telling them I was not an actor, especially when we had to repeat a scene. I could barely remember what had just happened in my life, never mind remembering how I felt so I could reenact it. I was a newbie opening a restaurant; I was stressed and exhausted, and the filming was very overwhelming. The director probably didn't mind: when I was most tired, I would emote more and there was more drama. I couldn't blame the crew. Their goal was to get some juicy emotions on film, whether that meant my emotional demise or not.

My only goal during the pilot filming was to open a restaurant and stay alive. But being on camera, I soon began to wonder what was real. When I was filming, I felt like I had two lives: the real one, and a parallel reality that was being altered through manipulation or editing to suit the crew's goals and time restrictions. They replayed my life in the way that suited them. I began to ask if reality was an illusion. Could it change depending on how an incident was portrayed or viewed through various lenses, or depending on an editing room cut?

We ended the first day of filming mostly excited about the process, and at the same time completely exhausted. We had given it our best shot, and now it was up to Mountain Road to prepare the cut and present it to the W Network for review. A few weeks later, just before Christmas, we were returning to Ottawa after visiting Dave's mom Irene in Brockville. His cell phone rang and it was Tim Alp congratulating us on a thirteen-part documentary-reality show: *The Restaurant Adventures of Caroline and Dave*. We looked at each other in disbelief, telling each other, "Merry Christmas!"

Then began a year of having our lives opened up to being filmed.

The crew had a key to our house so they could set up before we woke in the morning or came home in the evenings. They had a key to our restaurant, and located a small office there; besides, their production truck became a permanent fixture outside. The production assistant had access to our daily agendas. Nothing was too insignificant to tell them; you could never hide from them. We would often return home and not recognize parts of our house because they had been transformed into a set or studio. Crew members would arrive early in the morning with their large, noisy truck, waking our quiet neighbourhood.

The truck would park and run loudly right under our bedroom window while a team of about ten people in steel-toed construction boots tried to quietly and quickly bring heavy production equipment and accessories into the house, strategically setting up wiring and lighting and moving furniture around. A sting operation this was not, but they were mostly kind. We often had to wait a long time before they were ready for us to start our day— which was a little frustrating when waiting for morning coffee, though Dave soon had the crew trained to bring him a cup. Doing anything that was being filmed took ten times as long. The production team had to get approvals from business owners, obtain signed forms from people that would potentially be in the scene, assemble a crew, set up the scene well in advance of us arriving, and figure where and how to film. Then there was the matter of controlling us. We were like kittens at times, restless and bored. I had a habit of wandering off.

At the end of June 2009, we held the ZenKitchen soft opening. Friends and supporters were to provide us with feedback on our menu and give us a chance to practice. The day before, we were rushing around with one hundred and one things to do before opening. Contractors were finishing one task only to find that there was another problem they had to resolve. Friends came to our rescue by cleaning windows, sweeping floors, and putting together tables and chairs. At the back of house, we scrambled in a kitchen that looked like a war zone. We'd had constant problems and delays with the kitchen ceiling, and the contractors were still repairing it as we prepped for service. I kept running out to the store or market for something we had forgotten or that hadn't arrived in time from a supplier. We had attacked seemingly endless prep lists, but progress was slow because the food was new to all the cooks. And the wires, lights, and cameras were as indiscreet as an elephant; my not exactly confident staff was made more nervous because they were wired for sound. At many points during the day, I didn't think the opening would come together. I wanted more time and more sleep. It felt like we barely managed it.

Then there was the matter of the actual opening. I thought I had hired an experienced sous chef who could take care of all the organization, systems, supplies and staff, and get each of these ready well in advance. I thought we would collaborate. Instead, he wanted to be the boss of the kitchen and lacked the managerial and organizational skills I thought he had. He did excel at criticizing me for what I didn't know, and made it clear that I wasn't a "real" chef (which clearly meant being a man). He loved doing this in front of the camera. The night before opening we were in rough shape, and I put into high gear the skills that had served me well up until then and that would eventually help me succeed as a chef and restaurateur. I am organized, I can think quickly on my feet to solve problems, I can multitask and delegate, and I'm able to roll up my sleeves and overcome challenges.

Opening ZenKitchen required me to call upon all my life experiences. My years of meditation and yoga practice kept me balanced and calm through the storm. Many times I thought it would take a miracle for the restaurant to open and provide food to customers. Yet we made it work through a combination of courage, aplomb, community and vision. ZenKitchen has now closed its doors, and I'd departed as chef and owner before the restaurant finally lapsed in 2014. But I'm extremely proud of what it meant to the Ottawa community, to vegans and foodies, to the neighbourhood...and to me. Many stories and recipes collected here represent memories from those bustling, vivacious years of my life.

DEC · 63

KAYA YIPPEE YIPPEE YEAH

I came into this world at 2:27 pm on August 19, 1962 at St. Joseph's Hospital in Toronto. My mother Suzie said it was a hot summer day, and with the window open at the hospital she could hear the sounds of the Canadian National Exhibition close by. She named me Caroline after Princess Caroline and Caroline Kennedy. When I was asked my name as a child, I couldn't pronounce "Caroline," so I said "Kaya." This stuck, at least with my family. My uncle Roy loved singing to me in a Japanese cowboy sort of twang, "Kaya yippee yeah, yippee yeah, it's a Kaya yippee yeah." That would make me giggle, and still does. My mom gave me a Japanese middle name, Ruriko, which means *lapis lazuli,* a beautiful blue semiprecious stone considered the stone of total awareness. I doubt my mom knew this; she was enamoured with a Japanese movie star called Ruriko and wanted to name me after her.

My parents had hoped I would be a boy and were disappointed I was not. They already had a girl, my sister. They had bought hockey sticks in advance for the boy they imagined would come. When I arrived, I'm sure they were happy enough in having a new baby, but they were also secretly disappointed. I felt that constantly, so I tried to please, to gain their love.

I was a tomboy child, and I would do daredevil tricks like walking back and forth on our balcony railing, which overhung a long drop to the underground garage and pavement below. Passersby would often tell me to stop because it was dangerous and I could fall. I would look at them, pause for a while, then continue once they had passed. I loved the adventure and freedom of being physically active, roaming or hanging upside down.

I did my homework, and I was the good kid in school. I stayed after class to help the teacher wash brushes after art class. I read a book almost every day, impressing even the librarian. My parents didn't really care about all this, and whenever I showed my mom anything, whether it was an art piece with a gold star, an "A" grade, or a 9 out of 10 on my homework, she wouldn't say much. She did sometimes ask, "Why not an A+?" I understand now that this type of criticism was not unique to my mom; it was the same with many Asian mothers at that time. The culture said that asking for more would make children try harder and that not complimenting us would make sure we didn't become conceited.

One dish I remember most from my childhood is *sunomono* salad, which my mom made often to accompany our dinners. As a child, I wanted desperately to help her in the kitchen and, in her weaker moments, she would reluctantly nod "OK." I was eager to help her slice up the cucumbers very thinly with the large knife and squeeze them tightly to wring out their water, as I watched her do hundreds of times. But I could never live up to her high expectations. In the end she would get furious at me for not doing something right and I would run out of the kitchen sobbing.

It took me a long time to come back to making the *sunomono* salad. The first time I did it I was anxious, feeling my mother was right there to look over my shoulder and criticize my work. But I did it perfectly, to my standards. Perhaps if she was still around she would accept my making it, or perhaps not. Slicing the salad as an adult, I realized her approval didn't matter anymore. I was creating my own version. In the summer, I put this salad on the ZenKitchen menu. It was a light, fresh salad for hot, sultry days of summer spent sitting on the patio. I served it with chopsticks because it didn't seem right that people would eat it with knives and forks. That was my mother coming out. I found customers loved using chopsticks, eating my dish the way I as chef had recommended and the way Japanese culture asked them to do.

SUNOMONO SALAD
VEGAN AND GLUTEN FREE

Salad
¼ cup dried wakame (dried seaweed)
1 English cucumber, washed, and cut into manageable sections, with each section cut in half lengthwise and then into thin slices
Coarse sea salt

Dressing
½ cup rice vinegar
3 tablespoons agave
1 teaspoon grated ginger
Sea salt

Garnish
¼ cup roasted white sesame seeds
1 green onion, green part sliced thinly on a diagonal

Directions
- Soak the wakame in water for about five to ten minutes, or until soft, and drain well.

- Put the cucumber slices in a bowl and sprinkle coarse sea salt on top. Cover with cold water and knead the cucumber slices in the water for about one minute. Let sit for approximately five to ten minutes. Transfer the cucumber slices to a bowl one handful at a time, squeezing the cucumbers tightly for excess water.

- In a bowl, mix the rice vinegar, agave, ginger and add sea salt to taste. Adjust seasoning to your liking.

- *Put the seaweed with the cucumbers and add half of the dressing over the salted cucumber-seaweed mixture. Squeeze the cucumbers with your hands. Pour off the excess liquid and discard. Add the remaining dressing. To serve: put the salad mixture into individual dishes and garnish with slivers of green onion and roasted sesame seeds.*

Yields 4-6 servings

RENDEZVOUS

My father, George, was born in Campbell River, British Columbia. He spent most of his formative years on Rendezvous Island, just east of the much larger Vancouver Island, which my grandfather had purchased for a family homestead.

Grandpa Otomatsu came to Canada in 1902 from the Kobe area of Japan. In 1917 he sent away for a picture bride, and soon after, my grandmother Asa was travelling across the ocean from Hiroshima to Canada. Asa had lost her previous husband and had three small sons she could not support. Widowed and destitute, she put herself on the picture bride market. She came over with little, including no English, and according to my aunts she was totally naïve, coming from a populated city in Japan to a rustic smallholding on a remote island. She had hoped to send money to her sons but there was barely enough for own family. After the war, she could not find any trace of her children in Hiroshima; she could only assume they had perished during the bombing. She was heartbroken.

Otomatsu and Asa had seven children, one who died at birth. She taught all her children to cook, although the boys were busy with their father's fishing business. They worked hard each year to stock up the cold cellar with their small farm's harvest. Delicate, gentle, and quiet on the outside, she wasn't afraid of working hard, and she knew how to survive.

On December 7, 1941, World War II began. George was sixteen. A government boat pulled up to the island one day to say that Canada was at war with Japan, and his family had one hour to evacuate. With lunch on the stove, their livestock waiting to be fed, and their family dog watching nervously and barking at the government officers, the family stepped onto the boat that would take them to the Hastings Park holding stations in Vancouver. The officers said the family would come back, but they were never able to return to Rendezvous.

My grandfather and dad were two of the first men taken to the ghost towns, BC's Japanese internment camps. My dad had never visited Japan and spoke the language only roughly. His only connection to Japan was his features, his skin colour. Canadian citizens of Japanese descent were now considered enemies of the state. Japanese families lived in wooden shacks, including my grandmother and her children. But like she had many years before, not knowing what would happen to her, Asa made the best of a bad situation. The Japanese have a phrase, *shikatagani*, which means that something can't be helped; it is the way it is. My family said *shikatagani* in the camps and after the camps. They felt deeply ashamed and guilty for being different, for standing out, and that Japan was at war with Canada.

My grandfather had chosen Canada for a better life, and he had made one. He loved Canada. I feel the thing that devastated him most was not the government taking away his possessions, but the country he loved so much turning its back on him and saying he was no longer welcome. That rejection reminds me of a love relationship in which one person leaves or dies suddenly. He never really recovered from it.

After the war, the residents of the camps were given two options: to go to Japan or to stay in Canada and relocate. This was in part because their land, stores, and possessions had been sold or given away, which officials didn't want to admit. Otomatsu, thinking he was no longer welcome in Canada, decided it would be best to try to rebuild his family's life in Kobe. He didn't realize that the neighbourhood he had left long ago was torn apart by the war, and his family had all died. When he arrived with his family, including George, he realized they were equally unwanted in Japan, resented as "westerners." There was a story in the local paper about Otomatsu; local Japanese couldn't believe that the young man who had left for Canada came back to his home-town some forty years later. He looked sad in the picture and died shortly afterwards, in 1949, dispirited and without a true home.

My aunt Helen married in the camp, so she didn't go back to Kobe. She eventually ended up in Toronto with her husband, working at Nikko Gardens as a server and saving every penny so that she could bring her family over, one person at a time. She brought the younger children first. The older children, including my dad, found jobs to support their parents. George worked in the US Army base in Osaka, cooking with a brigade for hundreds every day. He was given cooking gear and an Escoffier cookbook, which I found many years later.

My dad, being second oldest, was one of the last to come back to Canada. He found a job as a cook for the workers at Leaver Mushrooms in Campbell-ville, Ontario, where he met my mom. He loved to cook for others, and to laugh and dance, and he was handsome. My mother was beautiful and had a charming smile. From this match and from mushrooms, I came to be.

Perhaps it is no wonder that I love eating and cooking with mushrooms, especially wild, earthy ones. When I was growing up, there was always some kind of mushroom in the kitchen. I remember the distinct smell of *shiita-ke* mushrooms and kombu soaking for a Japanese broth. I loved the sweet pickled *enoki* mushrooms we ate with hot rice. I watched as my mother marinated mushrooms for the futomaki roll she would make for special occasions.

I developed a creamy mushroom soup at ZenKitchen that had no cream and was packed with mushrooms and love. It soon became a customer favourite. The earthiness of the mushroom will always remind me of rootedness, the sort of good, rich knowing that I imagine Grandfather Otomatsu might have briefly captured on the Rendezvous homestead.

CREAMY MUSHROOM-ANCHO SOUP

VEGAN AND GLUTEN FREE

Ingredients

6 tablespoons olive oil

2-3 onions, peeled and chopped into a medium half-inch dice

¼ cup dry sherry

¼ cup rice flour

1 teaspoon ancho chili powder

4 cups porcini and shiitake stock (recipe follows) and chopped porcini and shiitake
pieces remaining

5 cups of button or cremini mushrooms, or a combination, cleaned and chopped

⅛ teaspoon grated nutmeg

2 teaspoons ground black pepper

2 teaspoons sea salt

Directions

◆ Clean and chop mushrooms and onions.

◆ In a pan, turn heat to medium and heat oil. Sauté onions over medium-low heat
   until they are tender and the skins are becoming translucent, about twenty to
   thirty minutes. Add sherry, reducing until almost dry. Add rice flour and ancho
   chili powder, stirring a few minutes. Lastly, add the mushrooms and stir them in.

◆ Add stock, one cup at a time, stirring to blend. Add porcini and shiitake pieces.
   Bring to a boil and then simmer for about twenty to thirty minutes.

◆ Puree soup in a blender or with a handheld immersion blender; return to pot.
   Add nutmeg and season to taste with more black pepper and salt. If you prefer
   a chunkier soup, do not blend the soup at the end. Or, you can blend half of the
   soup and return it to the pot.

PORCINI AND SHIITAKE STOCK

VEGAN AND GLUTEN FREE

Ingredients

1 cup dried porcini and shiitake mushrooms

4 cups boiling water

Directions

- Place the dried porcini and shiitake mushrooms in a medium-sized bowl and add four cups of hot water. Soak until softened, about thirty minutes.

- Strain the stock through a fine mesh colander, chopping the porcini and shiitake (remove stems) to add to the soup.

A BOWL OF RICE
IN THE MIDDLE OF THE NIGHT

What my mom loved more than anything was food: shopping for it, cooking for others, and eating. It was comfort for her, and she was happiest and most at peace when she was cooking. After she suffered a second stroke, she was partially paralyzed. She couldn't see or walk well, and talked with a slur. I recall meeting her once at the Japanese Canadian Cultural Centre in Toronto, where there was a festival and food was the focus as usual. She spent most of her life volunteering there and it was home for her. Someone had found a stool from where she could see all the action in the kitchen and she seemed happy. When she saw me, she called out my name, waving me over, then started telling me excitedly about what kind of food they had made for the festivalgoers. I felt her excitement about feeding people.

Although my mother and I both loved food, our relationship was complicated. Suyeko Ishii (nee Inouye), or Suzie as her friends called her, was born in the Celtic Cannery in Richmond, British Columbia on June 23, 1927. Her mother died when she was five and her father three years later. Their five children were sent in different directions, some to homes of relatives, one to an orphanage. It was decided that the youngest girl, Suyeko, would be sent to Japan to live with family members in the village of Shiidamachi in the Fukuoka-ken of Kyushu Island. She later referred to this place as the *inaka* or backcountry. It was very difficult for her to be uprooted from Canada to Japan. The culture was foreign to her and she longed to be with her brothers and sisters again.

After World War II, her brother Yosh Inouye found her and wanted her to come back to Canada. She was working at the US Army base in Tokyo as an administrator and translator because she knew English. He was living in Toronto and paid her way back. So, some twenty years after being sent to Japan, my mother made the trip back to Canada by boat. She was always different, an outcast, because although she was born in Canada she spent her teenage and young adult life elsewhere. She was like an *issei* or first generation Japanese-Canadian, but she was really a nissei or second generation. This is an important distinction in the community, which members are often curious to know. Although she was happy to be back in Canada, by then Japanese culture was more familiar to her, and she must have missed her friends. Certainly in the years after her stroke, she longed to go back to Japan to live, but she was too sick.

Suzie would sometimes wake up suddenly from night terrors, yelling out in pain. I ran to her to see what was wrong, and she told me snippets of her past. She was forced to stay in a dark house, alone with nothing to eat while her guardians were gone. They hit her. They made her work hard in the field all the time. They didn't want her. I would try to comfort her, but then all of a sudden her eyes would become hardened. She wouldn't remember what she had said. That was life with Suzie and her secrets, which went to the grave with her for the most part. She refused to get help for her pain, which naturally affected her life with me. I'm sure she didn't want to be the type of mother who let her anger and hurt from the past come up uncontrollably and unexpectedly in violent outbursts, wounding those around her. She loved me deeply but her past was too strong to overcome. Like an addiction, she often succumbed to what seemed natural to her—which was lashing out.

I did realize that my mom wasn't well when I was growing up but I didn't know what to do about it. I clung to the aspects of her that I could understand, and they often had to do with loving food. I would sometimes wake up in the middle of the night and go downstairs to find my mother awake with lights and music on, cleaning. I didn't understand why she was awake, but I didn't question it much; she seemed happy and peaceful, something I didn't see a lot during the day. When she realized I was watching her, she wouldn't scold but would welcome me as if she was expecting me. She'd put on the kettle for hot water, fill up our clay teapot with green tea, scoop some cold rice into bowls and find pickles to eat. When the hot water was ready, she would carefully put it into the teapot and then pour it over the cold rice, making *ochazuke*. We would eat the ochazuke with pickles.

While it may seem rudimentary to make foods like ochazuke, its making and eating evokes comforting memories in me that are priceless. When you attach memories to food, all the senses involved, whether of sights, sounds, touches or tastes, brings us home, even for a moment. I still love ochazuke, which is comfort food for many Japanese, served often with pickles and small servings of fish or meat. I've often said that rice is on the list of one of last things I would like to eat before I die. I believe every nationality and country has its own ochazuke, a food that brings back childhood comfort and memories of home. Rice and pickles transport me to eating a bowl of rice with my mother in the richness of the night.

Along with a recipe for the ochazuke, I'm providing my Aunt Betty's recipe for quick *takuwan* (pickled daikon), courtesy of my cousin Randy Okihiro. I served them at ZenKitchen on the Zen tapas plate.

OCHAZUKE

VEGAN AND GLUTEN FREE

Ochazuke is a simple dish made by pouring hot green tea, hot water, or dashi (stock) over cooked Japanese white rice and adding usually savoury toppings. Common toppings include umeboshi (salted plums), nori (dried seaweed), roasted sesame seeds, freshly grated ginger and wasabi (Japanese horseradish). It is a deceptively simple dish, but tasty, eaten by the Japanese as a quick meal or snack. It is also a favourite home comfort food, especially when accompanied by tsukemono (Japanese pickles).

Ingredients
Hot green Japanese tea—you can use the tea you prefer; my favourite is gen mai-cha (green tea with roasted rice)
Japanese cooked white rice (leftovers are usually used)
½ teaspoon gluten free tamari or soy sauce (optional)
Possible Toppings
Thinly cut roasted nori
Roasted sesame seeds
Freshly grated ginger
Wasabi
Umeboshi
Furikake (packaged Japanese seasonings to put on top of rice)

Directions
- *Put rice in a rice bowl and top with what seasonings you would like. Pour hot green tea over rice. Add a little soy sauce if you want.*
- *Serve with tsukemono. Itadakimasu!*

TAKUAN TSUKEMONO

VEGAN AND GLUTEN FREE

Ingredients

1 or 2 daikon (giant white radish), peeled and cut into thin half moons
2 Thai chili peppers, deseeded and cut into thin strips
2 teaspoons coarse sea salt
2 cups rice vinegar
1 ½ cups unrefined sugar
1 teaspoon turmeric

Directions

- Cut daikon and Thai chili peppers. For the sauce, combine rice vinegar, sugar, turmeric and salt well.

- Cover the daikon with the sauce in a pot. Quickly heat the daikon mixture but do not boil or the daikon will get too soft. Take off of the heat and let cool.

- The takuan (pickled daikon) will keep for at least a month in the refrigerator.

COOKIES FOR YOU

My mother always stocked our fridge with kielbasa and pirogies from the Eastern European delis near where we lived in Toronto. One particular day when I was about five, I went along with her to the deli. I wanted to be near the hustle and bustle of older, hefty women speaking languages that were not English. My mother entered the deli and there was a small crowd gathered around a plate of cookies that the manager had proudly put out to encourage tasters. My mother was excited, especially by free samples, and put her hand out to grab one. The manager said loudly, "Not for you!" All the women looked. She pulled her hand back, put her head down, grabbed my hand, and walked quickly out of the store.

I'm sure the store manager and women in the store that day have long forgotten that incident. It wasn't important for them. But I have never forgotten it, and I don't think my mother did either. She went back to the car with me and didn't say anything, but I saw her face and body shaken up and deeply hurt. I felt this in my heart. I didn't understand why those women were so mean to her. Over time, as I got older, I understood their prejudice. I've felt it countless times since then, of course, but that was the pivotal moment when I first intuited how words can wound someone deeply. These kinds of memories are not forgotten, but are like prints on our soul; they are our rites of passage, forming us in more ways than we know. When I was a child, everything looked so easy and sweet, but there were moments that, like this one, yanked me out of that sweetness. Without uttering a word, those women in the deli made me begin to question whether I was the same as other people.

As a chef, I often felt phony. The people I surrounded myself with, for the most part, told me that to be a chef I needed to speak with certainty and authority, have years of experience and act like a man. I resisted, I was defensive, and I was hurt. Now I know why: I didn't trust the process or myself, instead listening to critical voices inside and outside. I was passionate about doing things in a new way—a way that was more humane and collaborative than most brutal kitchen environments—but I was also a newcomer to back of the house stereotypes and was insecure about my role. No matter how many people praised my work or how many chef medals I got, I only listened to those who were critical because their voices resonated with my inner voice. It was a match. It's like the game *Concentration*, which I played when I was a kid. You had to guess which card went with another. I had all the cards before me, so many options to choose from, and I would hone in on one negative, critical, judgmental, and closed card. My questioning, and my constantly intuiting that I was somehow different or less than others, gave me an inferiority complex.

I've always found respite from this restlessness and self-questioning in baking and cooking. One of my childhood cookie recipes was an old-fashioned oatmeal cookie with brown sugar and fat rolled oats. I loved the transformation involved in baking and eating the cookies: combining ingredients as I mixed the batter, making rounds by pressing the balls of dough with a glass dipped in sugar, taking them out of the oven, and sharing them with others. I couldn't believe that I could be the conduit, the creator of this transformation, and I liked that.

I adjusted these cookies to be healthier than the original version, but they still retain their essence. They are meant for sharing, to be offered in kindness and unconditional love so that they can reverse mean-spirited actions. The recipe is for my mother. I wish I could press a cookie into her outstretched hand.

OATMEAL COOKIES

Ingredients
1 ½ cups unrefined brown sugar, firmly packed
1 ½ cups unsalted butter
3 cups large flake oats
1 ½ teaspoons baking soda
1 ½ cups unbleached flour, sifted

Directions
- Preheat oven to 350 degrees Fahrenheit. Mix all ingredients together well. Form dough into small balls about the size of small walnuts. Place on an ungreased baking sheet one inch apart.

- Butter the bottom of a small glass, dip in sugar and flatten the balls. Dip glass in sugar as necessary to keep from sticking.

- Bake in a 350 degree Fahrenheit oven for seven to ten minutes. Allow cookies to cool for a few minutes on a cookie sheet to firm them. Carefully remove with spatula. Cool.

Yields three to four dozen

JAPAN

My first trip to Japan in 1975, with my mother, deeply influenced my feelings about food. I was thirteen. Suzie also loved traveling and trying new cooking techniques and tastes. The whole trip was a sensory experience. She took me everywhere from a hotel in Tokyo to a shack in the backcountry of her childhood. We ate at ramen stands; we tried the food of local sushi masters; we tasted street food at the *obon* festival food stalls. All the while, she ate her way through a country and a cuisine that she missed so much. She wanted desperately to share the experience with me.

With each recipe I try, each place I go to eat, or each time I open up a cookbook, there is new information and knowledge being transferred that changes how I feel about food. And I learn the most about food when I travel. Seeing food in new and interesting ways helps me when I come home to appreciate everything afresh. I love the different kinds of ingredients that I get to try when traveling, but what fascinates me most is different cultures' approaches to shopping, cooking and eating, or even to recycling what's left over after a meal is prepared. In most places I've traveled outside North America, shopping for food is an important daily ritual in which vendors and buyers often know each other well. Eating together is another ritual: families sit together to share a labour of love alongside their experiences from the day. Seeing and experiencing these types of meals during my travels has touched me deeply.

That first trip to Japan resonated well into my adulthood, and by 1993 I had wanted to visit again for a long time. I had my second chance to experience Tokyo when I was a relief worker with the International Federation of Red Cross and Red Crescent Societies in Khabarovsk, Russia. I had developed a communications strategy for a media tour of the Russian far east in order for Japanese and international media to observe firsthand the social and economic situation in Khabarovsk, and to see the impact of Japanese and international humanitarian aid on the Russian people. The flight to Tokyo was only one hour and I was one of the first young foreign women invited to present at the Japanese Red Cross Society.

On my third visit to Tokyo, I was interning as a vegan chef. I stayed with Yuki Itoh, who I became good friends with while we were studying at the Natural Gourmet Institute, in the Yoyogi Park area of the city for a month, worked at her vegetarian restaurant, and experienced the city more fully. I have many more food memories from this trip.

It might seem evident when I say that I love Japanese food—I am, after all, of Japanese ancestry. But any assumptions about my having a "natural" affinity for Japanese culture or food would be wrong. This hasn't been always the case: I had to grow into my love of the cuisine. This is one of the reasons that I originally didn't want ZenKitchen to be in Chinatown. I thought people would assume that my food was Chinese, because many people assume that any Asian-looking person is Chinese. When we did eventually find the right place in Chinatown I remember someone highly educated saying to me, "Now you are with your people." What does that even *mean*? I felt offended. I am first and foremost Canadian. I was born here, my parents were born here, and if I *look* Asian, that doesn't make me have to *do* everything "Asian," including my cooking.

When I was working in marketing, an ex-colleague, a young man of Irish descent, said to me at a meeting in front of others, "I'm surprised you are wearing an Irish Claddagh." He made it sound like it was his birthright to wear the Claddagh, but certainly not mine. I replied, "I'm surprised that you are driving a Japanese car." He looked at me in an embarrassed way and that was the end of that. I could feel my colleagues smirking.

Even though I am firstly Canadian and secondly Japanese, and even though my professional food life was not in Japanese cuisine, the food of my mother's country is as dear to me as she is. One of the things we both adored was eating these *manju* cakes, soft cakes filled with red bean paste, while sipping on green tea.

MANJU

Ingredients

4 cups unbleached all-purpose flour

2 teaspoons aluminum-free baking powder

1 teaspoon baking soda

⅛ teaspoon sea salt

1 ½ cups unrefined sugar

4 eggs

½ cup milk

½ cup unsalted butter

2 teaspoons milk

Goma (sesame seeds)

4-5 cups anko (sweet red bean paste)—recipe follows

Directions

- Preheat oven to 425 degrees Fahrenheit.

- Melt butter and add sugar gradually. Add eggs one at a time beating well after each addition. Put aside the yolk of the last egg. Add milk and mix well.

- Sift flour, baking powder, baking soda and salt. Add flour mixture gradually into egg mixture.

- Spread out dough on floured surface. Roll out dough evenly to a ¼" thickness with a rolling pin. Do not knead the dough. Using a 2" circle cutter or glass, mark the dough so you know where to put the anko balls. Gather dough around each anko ball, pinching sides and folding in the ends to seal and make an oval shape Place on a baking sheet gathered side down.

- Beat egg yolk and two teaspoons milk. Brush on top of manju. Dip finger in goma and press gently on top of manju. Bake in 425 degrees Fahrenheit oven for seven to eight minutes.

Yields 4 to 5 dozen

ANKO

Ingredients
4 cups adzuki beans
3 cups unrefined sugar
2-inch piece of dashi kombu (dried seaweed for stock)
1 teaspoon sea salt

Directions

- Wash the beans and soak overnight in plenty of water. Drain.

- Put the beans in a pot with the kombu and cover with water. Bring to a boil and then simmer until beans are very soft, about one hour, and take out the kombu. Add more water when necessary to prevent the beans from drying out; the water should almost entirely be reduced when the beans are done. Near the end, stir in the sugar with a spoon. At the end, mix in the salt well. You want a thick mixture in which the beans are at least half crushed, thick enough to form balls about 1 teaspoon in size. If the mixture is too liquidy, drain with a colander.

- Make sure the anko is at room temperature before making manju, as it will take longer for it to bake in the oven when it comes straight from the refrigerator.

- If you have extra anko, it freezes well for later use and it's delicious with ice cream or yoghurt.

KOKORO

When I was young, I rebelled against my Japanese upbringing. I loved to eat Japanese cuisine at home, but was horrified if my mom packed something Japanese in my lunch. I would try to hide it before the other kids could see it.

I also took for granted that my mother could cook such wonderful Japanese food from scratch. I thought a lot of what she ate, like *sashimi* (raw fish) or *natto* (fermented soybeans) was strange or smelly. I was annoyed and embarrassed, thinking, "Why can't she eat eggs and bacon like other moms?" But when we first traveled to Japan together, I learned to prefer Japanese breakfasts over French-style breakfasts of eggs, strangely coloured, perfect, small sausages, lots of mayonnaise, and *pain* or bread.

As a guest in our host's home, I would be first to use the ofuro or deep bath, and got to eat the best of what the family could offer us for breakfast, which consisted of hot rice, nori sheets, miso soup, pickles and sometimes some grilled fish. At one house, the wife would warmly serve my mom and me breakfast while her six children patiently waited for us to finish. A child's face peaked quietly around the corner now and then, waiting for us so he or she could eat the leftovers. The mother ate last. This tradition made me grateful for the food I was given, stinky, strange or not.

There is nothing like eating food in the place where it was born to speak. Perhaps that's why I realized that food is more than food during my first trip to Japan. My mother introduced me to Japanese cuisine out of love: love for me, for the food, of course, and for the people making it, whether family, friends, or a street vendor. I watched as a cook in a *kimono* with *hachimaki* (headband) intently grilled corn on all sides, glazing it. He handed me my corn in a napkin with a big smile, saying *hi dozo* and bowing a little. It was delicious, the corn and the experience. After our trip to Japan, I came to love the food that my mom loved, and we would share in this addiction. She knew I couldn't resist *sushi*, so she would entice me to hang out with her by treating me to sushi meals. Food was our mediator.

Japanese food has had a strong influence on my own cuisine. My use of pristine ingredients, simple, clean, and subtle flavours, and elegant presentation are all inspired by Japanese culture. However, I have been most touched by seeing and tasting food as an offering from the feelings, personality, and heart of the cook. The Japanese word for this is kokoro.

For special occasions, my mother would make a special home-style sushi called futomaki, which is a fat sushi roll with carefully prepared fillings. I would love watching her make the sushi ingredients and roll the sushi, begging for any scraps she had to spare along the way. There was a magic ingredient in my mom's cooking that made you fall in love with the food immediately and want more, and many years later I realized it was kokoro. This recipe for futomaki is based on my mother's, but it has been adapted so that it's easier to prepare and is vegan.

FUTOMAKI

VEGAN AND GLUTEN FREE

Ingredients
Three sheets toasted nori
3 cups sushi rice (recipe follows for making Japanese white rice or brown rice)
Wasabi cream: using the sour cream recipe in this book, add a few tablespoons of wasabi to desired heat preference
Roasted sesame seeds
Possible Fillings
Pickled carrots (see recipe that follows)
Seasoned shiitake mushrooms (see recipe that follows)
Avocado, peeled, pitted and sliced, sprinkled with lime juice
English cucumber, deseeded, cut into thin strips
Red pepper, deseeded and cut into thin strips
Takuan (pickled daikon) cut into strips

Directions
- *Prepare a small bowl with water and a splash of rice vinegar to dip fingers into while making the sushi, so that it doesn't stick while you work.*

- *Lay a bamboo rolling mat onto your work surface and place a sheet of nori, shiny side down, onto the mat.*

- *Dip your hands into the finger bowl and place two big handfuls of rice at the centre of the nori, about one cup. Spread the rice evenly across the whole width of the nori, leaving about a one-inch margin uncovered on the long side, farthest from you.*

- *Spread the wasabi cream across the centre of the rice, sprinkle the sesame seeds over the cream, and layer desired fillings—at least three.*

- *Lay ingredients in the centre of the rice and other ingredients to the left and right.*

- *Place your thumbs under the rolling mat and lift the near edge of the mat with your thumbs and index fingers. Hold the fillings in place with the rest of your fingers.*

- *Holding a small flap at the top of the mat, bring the near side of the roll over so that it covers the fillings. Bring the rolling mat down to meet the strip of nori and gently squeeze along the length of the roll to tuck in the nearest edge.*

- *Lift the front edge of the mat slightly with your hand and use the other hand to gently push the roll forward, so that the strip of nori not covered by rice seals the roll. Pull back the mat and set it aside, seam down. With a sharp knife, cut roll into pieces just before eating. Serve with tamari or soy sauce and wasabi.*

SUSHI RICE

Ingredients
1 ⅓ cups Japanese short grain rice uncooked
1 ½ cups water
4-inch piece of dashi kombu
¼ cup Japanese rice vinegar
2 tablespoons unrefined sugar
½ teaspoon sea salt

Directions
- *Wash the rice thoroughly several times until the water becomes clear. Place the rice in a strainer to drain well. Place drained rice and water in a pot and set aside for thirty minutes or more.*

- *Put the washed rice and water in a pot. Put the dashi kombu on top and cover with a tight-fighting lid. Bring to boil, reduce heat and simmer for about fifteen minutes. Then remove from heat and stand for ten minutes with lid on.*

- *To make sushi vinegar, combine the vinegar, sugar and salt, stirring until the sugar dissolves. The mixture can be gently heated to dissolve the sugar and make the vinegar slightly milder, but do not boil. Set aside.*

- *Transfer the rice to a large container, preferably nonmetallic. Slowly add a little of the vinegar mixture at a time, folding in gently with a spatula. Not all the vinegar may be needed. Fan to cool, turning occasionally. Keep the rice covered to stop the rice from drying out while you are making the sushi.*

BROWN RICE SUSHI

Ingredients
1 ⅓ cups short grain brown rice uncooked
2 cups water
4-inch piece of dashi kombu

Directions
- *Rinse rice well and drain. Put the rice in a pot with the water and dashi kombu on top. Bring to a boil; reduce the heat to simmer and cook for about thirty minutes.*

- *Remove from heat and let stand ten minutes.*

- *Follow the same directions as for the white sushi rice.*

PICKLED CARROTS

Ingredients

2 medium carrots

¼ cup rice vinegar

1 teaspoon gluten-free tamari or soy sauce

½ teaspoon peeled and grated ginger

2 teaspoons unrefined sugar

½ teaspoon sea salt

Directions

- Peel and cut two medium carrots into thin matchsticks.

- In a small pot, combine the vinegar, tamari/soy sauce, grated ginger, sugar and salt. Heat up the mixture gently, stirring until the sugar dissolves, and then pour over the carrots.

- Refrigerate for a few hours. The pickled carrots will keep for one to two weeks in the fridge. Other vegetables can be substituted, such as celery and daikon.

SEASONED SHIITAKE MUSHROOMS

Ingredients
12 dried shiitake mushrooms
1 teaspoon maple syrup
1 tablespoon gluten-free tamari or soy sauce
½ teaspoon rice vinegar
Pinch sea salt
1 tablespoon sesame oil

Directions
* Put the mushrooms in a pot with water covering; bring to boil and simmer for twenty to thirty minutes. Drain the mushrooms, keeping the water to use as a stock.

* Discard the stems and slice thinly. Sauté mushrooms in a saucepan with sesame oil, maple syrup, tamari/soy sauce, rice vinegar, and a pinch of sea salt.

101 APPLE PIES

My sister and I once asked George to make us apple pie. He was something of a chef in his own right. We knew he could cook and cook fast, whipping up a breakfast of eggs, bacon, toast, and cereal in a few minutes. He enjoyed making simple food like fish or ground beef and rice, although he left most of the cooking to my mom. She made beautiful food and he had two full-time jobs.

Between three and eleven o'clock every day, George worked at a factory. Then he'd come back home to sleep, wake up early, and take care of gardening clients until the following afternoon. I seldom saw him except when I was very little and he would take me on gardening rounds. He said gardening was not girls' work, so I didn't do much except sweep the grass off patio stones. I played in the acres and acres of his customers' land, making up stories with my dolls. I also looked forward to seeing my dad if I was still awake when he came home from the factory, when he would sometimes make extra ramen with pickles for us to share; and I tried to sit with him when he had his daily ochazuke before beginning an afternoon nap. I never heard him complain about work or say that he was tired. It was his way of life to provide for his family, so he continued working even after the mortgage was paid off and my sister and I had left home.

We always knew my dad could make diner food but we never knew the extent of his cooking abilities. He did often speak about the delicious apple pies he used to make. One fall, my sister and I decided to call him on it. We bought lots of apples and the ingredients he needed, and we told him we would help him make the pies. We started peeling apples and he told us to keep going every time we asked if we were done yet. We didn't realize that my dad only knew how to cook apple pies in large quantities; he had learned while working for the US Army. He made tons of pastry dough and we scrambled through the house to find every container imaginable in which he could place the dough and fill it with apples. After the baking, our house was filled with what seemed like one hundred and one pies. We ate some, gave them to as many people as possible, and then ate some more. We never asked my dad to make apple pies again.

The great apple pie incident is a good snapshot of my dad in action. He enjoyed life and loved to have fun. He was present and grateful for everything. He didn't complain much and didn't store many regrets or resentments.

APPLE PIE

VEGAN

For the filling, I like to combine a variety of apples for their taste and texture. Some apples are tart and crisp and will keep their shape when baking, like Courtland and Braeburn, while others are sweet and soften as they are baked, like MacIntosh and Golden Delicious.

Ingredients

Pastry crust—see recipe that follows
6 cups apples, peeled and thinly sliced, covered with lemon juice
½-¾ cup unrefined sugar combined with an equal amount of unrefined brown sugar (total amount depends on the tartness of the apples)
2 tablespoons unbleached flour (optional)
¾ teaspoon cinnamon
½ teaspoon sea salt
⅛ tablespoon lemon juice

Directions

- *Heat oven to 425 degrees Fahrenheit.*

- *In a large bowl, stir together the filling—apple slices with sugar, cinnamon, salt and lemon juice. If the mixture is too liquid, pour out some liquid and/or sprinkle flour lightly on top of the apple mixture.*

- *Place the filling evenly into the piecrust. Top with the second crust, wrapping excess top crust under the bottom crust edge. Press edges together to seal and flute edges as desired. Cut slits in top crust to vent. Chill the pie for ten minutes to rest the pastry before baking.*

- *Bake first twenty minutes at 425 degrees F, then turn down the oven to 350 degrees Fahrenheit and bake another thirty to forty minutes or until the apples are* tender, the filling is bubbling through the slits in the top crust, and the crust is golden brown. If the crust starts to brown too quickly, put foil around the edges.

Yields one nine-inch pie

PASTRY CRUST

Ingredients
2 cups unbleached flour
1 cup shortening or butter (cold)
5-6 tablespoons ice water
$\frac{1}{2}$ teaspoon sea salt

Directions
- With pastry cutter, cut shortening/butter into flour until it becomes pea sized. Gradually add the ice water and mix in with a fork quickly and lightly until the dough is uniform and not sticky to your hands. Mound into a ball and cut in half. Cover each half with plastic wrap and chill twenty to thirty minutes in the fridge to rest the gluten.

- Sprinkle flour on a work surface and rolling pin. Unwrap the dough, sprinkle the dough with flour, and roll out the dough from the centre outward, ending with a circle about 12" in diameter and $\frac{1}{8}$" thick.

Yields pastry for the top and bottom of a nine-inch pie

THE MATTERHORN
AT YONGE-DUNDAS

My first job was at the Baskin-Robbins ice cream shop on Yonge and Dundas in Toronto when I was fifteen. I had no experience working, but a lot of enthusiasm and commitment. The manager must have sensed that when he decided to hire me. This was my introduction to working with food.

I was proud of the perfect scoop I developed over time. I could recreate it in form and weight at warp speeds, which was important when we got particularly busy. There were lineups out the door on most summer nights and even longer ones after a concert at Maple Leaf Gardens or Massey Hall. A manager from the corporate office would come in randomly to check our scooping techniques and weigh our cones. When we had a large lineup of customers, the biggest challenge was to quickly make a Matterhorn sundae with eight scoops of ice cream, a variety of sauces, a banana, nuts, cherries and lots of whipped cream to create its mountaintop.

I would arrive for my shift right after school, starved, and ice cream would be my dinner. This sounds ideal if you love ice cream, and I did, but after a year or so of eating ice cream for dinner, I couldn't eat it again for more than a decade. People would find my aversion to ice cream strange, but when I told them I could eat all the ice cream I wanted when I was younger, they looked at me with both pity and envy. I guess you don't know what it's like to have too much of a good thing until you do.

I did start to eat ice cream again, and I always chose vanilla. It is still one of my favourite flavours. I love it with chocolate chips. When I created desserts for my ZenKitchen pop-up dinners, I often tried various vegan ice creams. I once served a cardamom-pistachio ice cream with orange-ginger sauce that friends still talk about some years later.

CARDAMOM-PISTACHIO ICE CREAM

VEGAN AND GLUTEN FREE

Ingredients

3 cups coconut milk, refrigerated overnight in cans

¾ cup maple syrup

¼ cup brown rice syrup

Pinch sea salt

1 teaspoon cardamom, finely ground

½ cup pistachios, chopped finely

Directions

- Put the cans of coconut milk in the fridge overnight.

- Combine coconut milk, maple syrup, rice syrup, salt and ground cardamom in blender. Process in blender until well blended. Add chopped pistachios into mixture and stir.

- Pour cooled mixture into ice cream machine and churn for twenty to twenty-five minutes, until creamy and somewhat firm.

Yields about 34 ounces

ORANGE-GINGER SAUCE

Ingredients

1 ½ cups of orange juice
¼ cup maple syrup
1 tablespoon arrowroot
1 teaspoon orange zest
1 tablespoon finely grated ginger

Directions

• In a small saucepan, bring 1 ½ cups of orange juice and maple syrup to a boil.

• In a small bowl, dissolve the arrowroot in two tablespoons of cold water, making a slurry. When the orange juice mixture boils, stir in the slurry. Be sure to stir continuously.

• Take off the heat, and stir in the orange zest and grated ginger. Cool.

Yields about twelve ounces

Notes:

Arrowroot is a fine-grained, white starch that comes from the root of the tropical arrowroot plant. It is an excellent thickener and better to use than cornstarch, which is highly refined. It is easily digestible, nutritive, and high in calcium.

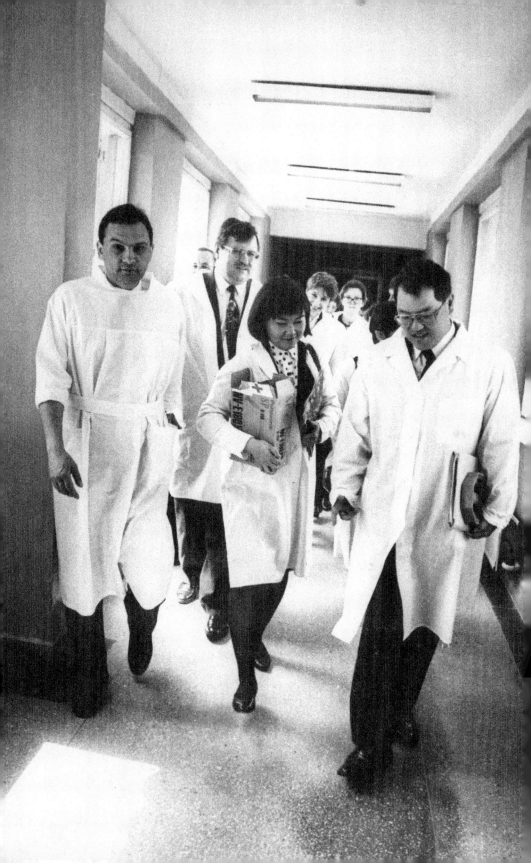

TO RUSSIA WITH LOVE

I had one of the best experiences of my life as a Red Cross relief worker throughout the Former Soviet Union from 1993 to 1994. I was on a humanitarian mission to support the delivery of medical supplies to the elderly, children in orphanages, women and babies in maternity hospitals, and babies in women's prison nurseries. Most of the imprisoned women had endured severe abuse from their husbands and eventually murdered them. Widespread problems—spousal abuse, alcohol addiction, and sexual assault—were rampant but not considered issues. In fact, it was only in 1993 that Moscow opened its first rape crisis centre, under much controversy.

I had many conversations with people even though we didn't share a common language. I held the hands of old people and listened to their stories, though I understood very little. The listening and the caring was the important part. In the orphanages, children looked at me solemnly. I knew they had already come from a lifetime of heartache and pain. We would bring toys and try to play; the kids would smile for a second or two, but what they really wanted was for me to take them home. I felt helpless and sad. It was heart wrenching when I left, watching the children watching me through the barbed wired fences of a sparse playground.

I was fortunate that work colleagues would bring me into their lives despite my limited knowledge of Russian. They tried to use every English word they learned from TV. *Dallas* was popular; so was the BBC News. Most of the time, though, our interactions required little or no words.

In the Ukraine, while en route from Kiev to the other side of the country by car, the driver said he wanted to make a short detour to say hello to his *babushka* at her *dacha*, a small cottage in the country. She was very happy when she saw us and insisted we eat some of her borscht, which was made with the vegetables from her dacha garden. It was a simple soup, nothing special if you looked at it, but when I tasted it with her watching me intensely, I could feel the love she put in it. The deliciousness of the soup and the love between her and her grandson touched my heart deeply and made me cry in joy. I looked at her, and said in my broken Russian, *"o-cheen' fkoos-ni,"* to which she smiled and nodded. She looked back at her grandson eating, from whom she wanted the ultimate approval.

I also remember fondly gatherings in the Red Cross office for a birthday or graduation celebration. We ate lots of food with *shampanskoye*, a local sparkling wine. When I sat down at one party, the table was filled with bowls of *pelmeni*, fresh dumplings served with sour cream. Those dumplings are one of my favourite foods and I was in heaven. At ZenKitchen, my memories of being in the Ukraine inspired me to create a vegan version of the dumpling filled with sauerkraut and a cashew-based sour cream.

TO RUSSIA WITH LOVE

SAUERKRAUT DUMPLINGS WITH SOUR CREAM

VEGAN

Ingredients

1 jar or can sauerkraut, drained and chopped into small pieces
1 package dumpling/gyoza wrappers (round shape)
Small bowl with water
Vegan sour cream (recipe below)
Chives, minced

Directions

* Place about a teaspoon of the sauerkraut filling in the center of each dumpling skin. Dab a little water around the edge of the skin. Fold over the skin to make a half-moon shape and use the thumb and index finger of one hand to press edges together firmly to make a tight seal. Ensure each dumpling is completely closed.

* Place the finished dumplings on a baking sheet lined with parchment paper. In a large pot, heat water until there is a gentle boil. Add some dumplings and, when they pop up to the surface, remove with a slotted spoon and arrange on a serving platter. Serve with sour cream sprinkled with minced chives.

Notes:

To freeze the dumplings for later use, lay them on a tray, lined with parchment paper, and place them in a freezer for a couple of hours or overnight. When they are frozen solid, you can place them in freezer bags. When ready to cook, remove as many as needed and drop them into the boiling water without defrosting.

CASHEW SOUR CREAM
VEGAN AND GLUTEN FREE

Ingredients
½ cup unsalted raw cashews
¼ cup apple cider vinegar
1 cup filtered water
½ teaspoon sea salt

Directions

• Soak the cashews in filtered water overnight or for a few hours. Drain.

• In a blender, combine the cashews, the apple cider vinegar, and ½ cup of water. Slowly add the remaining water until it becomes creamy. Season with sea salt to taste.

WHAT I KNOW IS
THAT I DON'T KNOW

I don't go to therapy to find out if I'm a freak;
I go and find the one and only answer every week.
It's just me and all the memories
to follow down any course that fits within a fifty minute hour...
When I talk about therapy, I know what people think:
that it only makes you selfish and in love with your shrink.
But oh how I loved everybody else
when I finally got to talk so much about myself.

—Dar Williams, "What Do You Hear in these Sounds"

I came back to Ottawa after my mission to Russia and Ukraine, broken and exhausted after a terrifying head-on collision near Lugansk between our Red Cross car and a tractor tailor —a near-death experience that made me grateful for my life but left wondering why I was saved and what I was to do.

When I left for Russia, I had a cat and a lovely house I shared with my boyfriend, who didn't want me to go away. Returning, I didn't know if we had a relationship anymore. Despite our unconfirmed status, we continued to live in the house together. I felt confused and lost.

All Red Cross delegates are encouraged to go into counseling after their missions, to debrief and reacclimatize. I was hesitant at first; I felt that seeing someone meant I was broken, not good enough, that I couldn't handle life. Nevertheless, I began seeing a therapist.

What I knew was that I didn't know. Many helping professionals and healers will tell you this is a good place to be, however difficult. From a place of not knowing, you have the humility to explore. In my sessions, I found out that I was laden with guilt from childhood about nearly everything, including going to therapy! That guilt was self-punishment. The more I hid from my problems and tried to suppress them, the more they came back at me, tugging at my pant leg, asking for attention and help. I had to become harsher and more aggressive not to hear the calm but desperate voice inside of me that was trying to tell the truth. Having the opportunity to talk and listen to myself, without judgment or criticism, was liberating.

During a session, I realized I always breathed shallowly. This is common in children from abusive childhoods, who live in a constantly anxious, fearful mode. That was a revelation for me. My therapist recommended yoga and meditation. At first, when I focused on my breathing, I felt that I couldn't breathe at all, that I was suffocating. I became desperate for breaths. It's fascinating how the breath and emotions are so connected, intertwined.

I took my first yoga class at twenty-nine. At first, breathing along with yogic asanas in class seemed like a lot of work. But I became calmer. By the end of the class, after *savasana* or corpse pose, I was in bliss. Despite the postures that were sometimes difficult and painful, in practising yoga, I was certainly calmer and more relaxed. I felt that I had come home.

I had been interested in meditation for a while but didn't know how to approach it, how to start. I began with a guided meditation, sitting in whatever way was comfortable, against a wall or in a chair. It was really scary and hard for me to sit for a few minutes at first and close my eyes; it seemed like an eternity and a jail sentence. But every day I did it, and the minutes built up over time, like doing training for a marathon. If you try to run the race without the

WHAT I KNOW IS THAT I DON'T KNOW

training, you collapse and fail. The same with meditation. If you try to do it with force, pushing yourself to go the maximum number of minutes, sitting in uncomfortable positions that make your legs cramp badly, and trying to replicate yogi meditators, it's too hard, too painful.

I still try different meditation techniques, environments, and positions. I say mantras, or don't. I focus on an object, on my breath, on my body. I change the number of minutes, the number of times a day. But the main thing is that meditating daily helps me enormously. Meditation is an opportunity to ramble and reflect on how I am feeling, much like therapy.

I can't express how much meditation, yoga, and therapy have given me. I wonder now why we don't all reach for them instead of the crutches that are harmful and destructive. When I went to my first yoga classes, I was amazed at my deep state of relaxation after savasana. The world seemed better, lighter, and more beautiful. In this state of bliss, my friend Barb and I would go to a local café by the water and share a large Caesar salad. I don't know if it was the yoga, the friendship, the food, or a combination of the three, but those were the best Caesar salads. I had to put a vegan Caesar on the ZenKitchen menu to honour the post-yoga feeling Barb and I shared during our café visits.

NEW CAESAR SALAD
VEGAN AND GLUTEN FREE

Ingredients
2 cloves garlic peeled, sliced

1 tablespoon miso

2 tablespoons lemon juice

1 ½ tablespoons balsamic vinegar

1 tablespoon Dijon mustard

1 teaspoon gluten-free tamari or soy sauce

1 teaspoon capers

⅓ of soft tofu block, drained

½ cup extra virgin olive oil

¼ teaspoon sea salt

¼ teaspoon freshly ground pepper

1 head romaine, cut or torn into bite size pieces, or other greens

½ cups carrots, peeled and shredded

Directions
+ In a blender, combine garlic, miso, lemon juice, vinegar, mustard, tamari/soy sauce, capers, and tofu. Add in oil slowly and blend until mixture is smooth and creamy. Add salt and pepper.

+ Add dressing to greens and carrots and mix thoroughly, adding only enough dressing to lightly coat leaves. Toss salad lightly with croutons.

Yields six to eight servings

WHAT I KNOW IS THAT I DON'T KNOW

SPICED CROUTONS

Ingredients
1 loaf of bread, preferably day old, gluten-free or regular

2 garlic cloves, minced

½ cup extra virgin olive oil

½ teaspoon or more sea salt

1 teaspoon smoked paprika

¼ teaspoon cayenne pepper

½ tablespoon ground cumin

½ tablespoon chili flakes (more or less, depending on desired level of heat)

Directions
- Preheat oven to 325 degrees Fahrenheit.

- Slice bread into half-inch slices. Cut slices into half-inch strips, then into half-inch cubes.

- In a deep bowl, toss bread cubes with olive oil, sea salt, garlic, and spices until each cube is well coated.

- Spread cubes in a single layer on a baking sheet. Bake until crisp and evenly brown (about fifteen to twenty minutes), turning often. Remove and set aside to cool. The croutons will last for two weeks.

THE DREAM NEVER DIES, JUST THE DREAMER DOES

By 2004, I was yearning for a new career, a new direction, but I still couldn't figure out what. It was frustrating: I was almost there, so close to finding out.

I took several courses, including a life mission course at the Kripalu Yoga and Health Center in Lennox, Massachusetts. I was envious of people who had breakthroughs during the workshop and figured out that they wanted to become a dancer, artist, or engineer. After looking at my life and talents, I came up with three words that my next career needed to have: passion, connection, and creativity. Those words were on my screen saver, I had them on my desk, I wrote them constantly in my journal, and they were on my mind all the time. But nothing concrete surfaced; it seemed the more I tried, the more I grasped, the more whatever I was searching for disappeared in the space between my fingers.

One day, I got a postcard from Kripalu for a workshop with Julia Cameron of *The Artist's Way* fame. I had been given the book long ago, or perhaps I'd bought in a garage sale. The quote from Cameron on the postcard read, "You are never too old to live your dreams." That resonated with me, and I registered for the course. It was a rare moment of just knowing, very clear and compelling.

I loved Cameron's methods for clearing blocks to our creativity. During the workshop, we spoke about our dreams, and out of the blue, my dream of owning a restaurant resurfaced. That idea had come up randomly for years when I had time to rest and reflect, but my critical mind suffocated it. It was also there that I started writing three pages upon waking called the morning pages. I found it was amazing what came out before my mind had the time to wake up and think about what was being written. A weekly artist date was another magical part of her equation. This is a solo activity, a one-hour adventure each week. I went out into nature for walks, cycled to the beach and walked on the rocks, or went to a coffee shop to write.

I had unlocked the dream of owning a restaurant. But it was now some twenty years from when I first wanted this, and I had changed. How could my dream of being a restaurant owner match up with the latest Caroline? I thought that I needed to rebuild from who I was, from my experience, from my skills. But in fact I needed to turn back to my memories and dreams. Writing in the morning, the dream of the restaurant got past the guards, the ego mind. The key was in a homecoming, not a reinvention. I'd tried to figure out my purpose through other means: prominent and high-paying jobs, promotions, fancy clothes, important friends or even travel. The harder I tried, the more depressed I became that I would never be truly content in a job.

During my stays at Kripalu, I came to love their thumbprint cookies, which now remind me of this period of self-discovery. There were few treats at the centre, so I would buy a cookie every night and savour it. They were freshly baked every day and there were only a limited number, so you had to be there at the right time to get one. I loved that they were handcrafted with a thumb imprint for the sweet jam centre, which balanced out the grainy wholesomeness of the cookie itself. The cookies had an impact on me: I started to realize that something could be good for our bodies and delicious too. I also recognized that there was fun in that cookie, which was a bit of a revelation. I started to wonder why food is usually only made to be fun for children. Food, much like the process of self-exploration, should be full of fun and curiosity.

THUMBPRINT COOKIES

VEGAN AND GLUTEN FREE

Ingredients

1 cup gluten-free oats, ground, or use quinoa flakes but do not grind

1 cup pecans or other nuts, ground

1 cup brown rice flour

½ teaspoon cinnamon

⅛ teaspoon ground nutmeg

⅛ teaspoon sea salt

½ cup coconut oil, melted

½ cup maple syrup

1 teaspoon vanilla extract

½ cup fruit jam, any flavour

Directions

♦ *Preheat oven to 350 degrees Fahrenheit.*

♦ *Pour the ground oats or quinoa flakes, ground nuts, flour, cinnamon, nutmeg and salt into a medium bowl.*

♦ *Whisk the oil, maple syrup and vanilla extract in a small bowl until well blended. Pour into the dry mixture and stir with a rubber spatula until the dough holds together when squeezed.*

♦ *Shape the dough into one-inch balls and place each ball one inch apart on ungreased baking sheets. Use your thumb to make an indentation in the centre of each cookie. Spoon a half teaspoon of jam into each indentation.*

♦ *Bake for fifteen to seventeen minutes or until the cookies are light brown on the bottom. Cool the cookies on the baking sheet for a few minutes until they are firm enough to move. Transfer them to a rack to cool.*

Yields two dozen cookies

CHEMAINUS

My dad and Aunt Helen would never travel by plane, but when they heard my Uncle Rondy in Chemainus, British Columbia was sick, they packed their bags and went to see him immediately. I went with them because I wanted to meet my uncle for the first time, and because they needed a driver. We stayed in a low-budget motel, and I in a bed with my aunt. My dad slept with Rondy, who usually lived on a fishing boat in the Chemainus harbour. I didn't understand then what was wrong with him; he seemed OK. He said he had stomach problems, but I later found out he was dying of stomach cancer.

My aunts and uncles woke up at the crack of dawn and waited outside the bedroom for me so they could go to breakfast. The motel kitchen was closed, but they wanted to get there early, be the first in line. Although they were in their seventies, retired, and had lots of time on their hands, they were never content with being idle and hated waiting in lineups. That was the Ishii way. I could hear their chatter outside my bedroom as I was trying to sleep in past five in the morning.

"Is she awake yet? Not good to sleep in so late. You think something's wrong with her, George? Should we wake her up? Gotta go for breakfast soon, don't want to be late."

There was a lull, and then the conversation started again. One of them came into my room, and I pretended to be sleeping. They reported back to the group: "She's still sleeping. I don't know how she can sleep like that. It's not good for you to sleep that much. Should I wake her up?" As soon as my hand had turned the knob to open the door, they stood up with their jackets, caps, and shoes on, and were out the door.

Aunt Helen and I slept together in the same bed on that trip. I'd creep into bed so as not to disturb her sleep. She told me often that she slept poorly and stayed up half the night reading. One night, instead of sticking her nose in a book, she started telling me things about herself and our family that I never heard before. We were timeless in that bed, like two teenagers, giggling, getting sleepy, talking some more, giggling.

She really surprised me at times. Once, visiting with family, she saw a stack of wood outside and bounded out to cut and stack it. There she was, in a long raincoat covering her dress, rain bonnet on, using the ax confidently and splitting wood. She was kind, softhearted, and generous, but at the same time very strong, confident, bold, and quirky. When she opened a jar of stinky Japanese takuwan pickles, she would say, "Smells like someone did something in their pants." If I dwelled on something too long, she said, "Move along." She volunteered a lot with her church and community. Even in her eighties, she would go out to help "older" people, bringing food and helping them with their chores.

Another aunt, Betty, was an excellent cook. Betty and Helen both loved making cabbage rolls, and I particularly remember making them with Aunt Betty. I loved how simple and fun it was to take simple ingredients like cabbage from her garden and fresh tomato sauce, creating a dish that was so filling and comforting. To this day, I still love cabbage rolls, and I served them once on a ZenKitchen tasting menu.

CABBAGE ROLLS

VEGAN AND GLUTEN FREE

Ingredients
1 large head cabbage or 2 medium heads cabbage

Filling
3 tablespoons olive oil
2 cups onion, finely diced (about 2 medium onions)
4 garlic cloves, minced
1 teaspoon chili flakes (more or less depending on heat preference)
1 teaspoon dried thyme
1 teaspoon paprika
1 teaspoon sea salt
1 teaspoon freshly ground pepper
1 24-ounce pack tempeh, coarsely grated
1 ½ cup carrots, coarsely grated
1 ½ cups short grain brown rice
1 tablespoon gluten-free tamari or soy sauce
1 tablespoon apple cider vinegar
1 tablespoon maple syrup
½ cup parsley finely chopped

Sauce
1 28 ounce can crushed tomatoes
1 28 ounce can chopped tomatoes, with their juice
1 tablespoon balsamic vinegar
2 tablespoons unrefined sugar
2 bay leaves
½ cup red wine
Sea salt and freshly ground pepper

Directions

- Preheat oven to 350 degrees Fahrenheit.

- To prepare the cabbage leaves, first core the cabbage(s) with a sharp paring knife. Bring to boil a large pot with water. Carefully place the cored cabbage in the hot water. Using tongs, gently transfer the outer leaves of the cabbage to a colander as they blanch and come off easily when ready. Rinse the leaves with cold water. Spread on towels and pat dry.

- To make the filling, put oil in a sauce pan over medium-high heat. Add the onions and cook until caramelized, about fifteen to twenty minutes. Add the garlic and spices and stir for a few minutes. Stir in the tempeh and cook for few minutes. Add the carrots and rice.

- To make the sauce, put the tomatoes, red wine, and bay leaves in a pot over medium heat. Bring to boil and then simmer for twenty minutes. Near the end, add the vinegar and sugar and simmer, stirring for a few minutes. Adjust the seasonings to taste and remove from heat.

- Prepare the baking dish. Put a thin layer of the tomato sauce at the bottom of the dish. Place one layer of blanched cabbage leaves on top of this.

- To make the rolls, lay the cabbage leaves, rib side down, on a flat work surface. Run a rolling pin over them to crush the spine. Spoon the about ¼ cup or more of the filling onto each leaf just above the stem. Fold end and sides over filling and roll up. Place the finished rolls, seam side down, on the sauce and cabbage leaves in the baking dish. Repeat with the remaining ingredients.

- Pour the remaining sauce over the rolls, ideally to half way up the side, and cover tightly with aluminum foil.

- Bake for about one and a half hours, until the leaves are softened.

- Remove from the oven and let sit for fifteen minutes before serving. Serve the rolls with the sauce spooned over the top and with vegan sour cream on top or on the side.

Yields about eighteen rolls

"NO SUCH THING AS TOO MUCH BUDDER!"

I had a vision for a restaurant where the food was not only beautiful and delicious but at the same time healthy for people and the planet. I didn't know how I would do that. I wasn't a chef, only a good home cook. All of my experience in restaurants had been in the front of house. I realized that I needed to take professional chef training. How would I know if a chef needed to buy this or that? What if the chef didn't come in or quit, what would I do? If this was to be my restaurant, I would have to take charge of the food.

During one artist's date, I went to Le Cordon Bleu Ottawa Culinary Arts Institute to watch a class. The school, the students, the white chef coats and hats impressed me—all were so...*French*. I watched intently as the chef teacher did a demo for about sixty students in neat rows of white. He was making a chicken with butter, and then there was rice with butter, and vegetables with butter, and of course a sauce with butter. At one point, one of the woman students raised her hand and asked what we were all probably thinking: "Why so much butter, Chef?"

The chef's face reddened and his lips turned from neutral to pouty as he said loudly in a French accent, "There's no such thing as too much budder. Budder is one of the food groups. You need budder!"

You could see the student cringing in her chair, and the tall hats of the students moved slightly as they tried to glance over at her inconspicuously. There was silence for a few moments, and then the chef went on cooking with plenty of "budder." I felt sorry for the girl and I also knew this school wouldn't be a good match for me.

During my time at Natural Gourmet Institute for Health and Culinary Arts, where I ended up training in the kind of health-conscious cooking I wanted to undertake, we had weeks on end where we would bake every day and be giddy with sweet, carbohydrate-filled tastings. The teacher would make a big pot of miso soup for lunch, saying that the saltiness and earthiness balanced all the sweets in our system. Miso soup has been used for centuries in Japan as a healing food. It is miso's combination of ingredients and its unique double-fermentation process that transforms soybeans into a potent medicine that combats all kinds of ailments—including, I guess, those that come from eating too much sugar and butter.

MISO SOUP WITH ENOKI MUSHROOMS

VEGAN AND GLUTEN FREE

Ingredients

9 cups of water

4-inch piece dashi kombu

12 dried shiitake mushrooms

2 tablespoons gluten-free tamari or soy sauce

2 tablespoons mirin (sweet Japanese cooking wine) or agave

½ teaspoon sea salt

¼ cup dried wakame, and 3 cups of cold water for soaking

1 package enoki mushrooms, trimmed

5 tablespoons miso (use the type you prefer; the lighter the miso, the sweeter, and the darker, the saltier)

Green onion, with the green section cut thinly on a diagonal

½ block soft tofu, cut into small ½-inch cubes

Directions

* Fill a pot with 6 cups of water; add kombu and dried shiitake mushrooms, and bring to a boil. Reduce to simmer. After simmering for about thirty minutes, remove the mushrooms, cut off and discard the stems, and thinly slice the caps. Return the mushrooms to the pot. Take out the kombu and discard. Reserve the liquid.

* Put wakame in a bowl with three cups of cold water and let stand to reconstitute and soften, about five to ten minutes. Strain the wakame with a colander, keeping the liquid and adding it to the kombu mushroom liquid.

* Bring the liquid to almost boiling and then reduce the heat to simmer. Add the tamari or soy sauce, mirin, and salt. Make a slurry with the miso dissolved in some hot broth and put in the pot. Place the wakame, tofu cubes and enoki in soup bowls. Pour the hot soup over. Garnish with green onions and serve.

NEW YORK, NEW YORK

I had seen ads in *Vegetarian Times* for the Natural Gourmet Institute for Health and Culinary Arts in New York City but had not given it much thought because it was too expensive. Then, preparing for a trip to San Francisco, I asked my friend Alfredo who was familiar with the dining scene in the city where to eat. He said to try out Millennium—the food was incredible, and by the way, also vegan.

Dave and I weren't vegetarian at the time but we wanted to try Millennium. We fell in love with it. The restaurant was beautiful, the philosophy to be as sustainable, local, seasonal and conscientious as possible in the buying and making of food. Its cuisine was creative, beautiful, and delicious, the ultimate criteria for me. Chef Eric Tucker came to our table at the end of our meal to talk about where some of the ingredients came from. We both loved that interaction; in fact, it was a pivotal moment. I realized how important it was, to the customer and the restaurant, to have this conversation. If you went to a friend's place for dinner, you would know who cooked the food and you could ask questions. I never understood why you didn't get the same chance in a restaurant.

Soon after, looking through the Millennium cookbook, I saw that Chef Eric was a graduate of the Natural Gourmet Institute. I was sold.

Dave and I were soon heading to New York City for a mini-vacation, and I had an appointment to visit the Natural Gourmet Institute. I met with the admissions director, who took me on a tour of the school. The classrooms were professional, and everyone was in chef gear; but there was lightness in what they were doing. The energy in the room was positive. They were focused but there was room for laughter. I watched a baking class and was encouraged to take part in tasting what they'd made.

The food was beautiful although vegan and healthful. I couldn't believe it. And once I tasted the deliciousness with the students giggling softly around me from their sugar highs, I fell in love with the food and school. I signed up shortly afterwards for the fall session.

LEMON CAKE

VEGAN

Adapted from a Fran Costigan recipe

Ingredients

1 cup unbleached white flour
1 cup whole wheat pastry flour
1 ½ teaspoons aluminum-free baking powder
1 teaspoon baking soda
¼ teaspoon turmeric
½ teaspoon sea salt
⅓ cup extra virgin olive oil
¾ cup maple syrup
⅔ cup non-dairy milk
¼ cup fresh lemon juice
2 teaspoons minced lemon zest
1 teaspoon vanilla extract
2 teaspoons lemon extract
2 teaspoons apple cider vinegar

Lemon Syrup

½ cup unrefined sugar
½ cup lemon juice
2 teaspoons lemon zest

Directions

- Preheat oven to 350 degrees Fahrenheit. Oil cake pan.

- Sift the flours, baking powder, baking soda, turmeric and salt. Stir with a whisk to distribute ingredients.

- *Whisk the oil, maple syrup, milk, lemon juice, zest, vanilla and lemon extracts and apple cider vinegar in a separate bowl until well blended.*

- *Pour the wet into the dry ingredients and stir with a whisk until the batter is smooth.*

- *Put the batter into the pan. Smooth the top with a spatula and tap the pans lightly on the counter to eliminate air bubbles.*

- *Bake for twenty minutes until the top is golden brown, a toothpick in the centre comes out clean, and the edges start pulling away from the sides of the pan.*

- *Allow the cake pan to cool for 15 minutes on a rack.*

- *For the lemon syrup, heat up in a small pot, the sugar, lemon juice and zest until the sugar dissolves.*

- *Remove the cake from the pan and set it on a rack set over a tray; spoon the lemon syrup over them. Allow the cake to cool completely.*

CHEF SCHOOL

Entering chef school was a new world. I needed vocabulary like *brunoise, mirepoix, chiffonade,* and "blanch and shock." I was graded on how fast and accurately I could chop and how well I could create flavours. Up to then I had largely been at a desk, either at an office or in my home. I was graded on strategic thinking or analysis. Now I was on my feet all day, following strict rules of conduct for what to do and not to do in a kitchen.

I loved the mindfulness of being in the kitchen. I needed to be there, in the now, to cook well. I wasn't in a meeting texting or doodling or thinking about what I was going to make for dinner that night. Being in a kitchen prevents sleepiness. Kitchen environments have very hot stove elements and sharp objects. People work in a tight space, and being mentally vacant is dangerous. Thus the no-nonsense language chefs use.

"Hot behind you!"

"Sharp knife!"

"Get the fuck out of the way!"

I wasn't above swearing if I was holding a large, scalding pot or sizzling hotel pan and someone wouldn't get out of the way.

I was one of the oldest students. Some students hadn't cooked or tasted much. The thought of becoming a chef looked like a cool job and most watched too much Food Network. I hadn't thought I had much to bring to the kitchen table, but actually, I had maturity and food experience. I had cooked a lot, and had tasted many different food creations in places all over the world, from the finest dining restaurants to meals made by home cooks or from roadside stands.

We had to prepare a graduation dinner with our team for our final grading. This dinner is served on Fridays at the school, which is transformed into a restaurant and opened to the public. Guests eat at communal tables and bring their own wine or beer. Our team ranged from twenty to sixty years old and our backgrounds and expertise were just as diverse: African, Japanese, Indian, and me, from Canada with Japanese roots. We decided to embrace our diversity and created a menu that showcased Indian and Japanese elements with a focus on the freshest ingredients and home cooking in an elevated way. It was amazing.

This recipe is from the graduation dinner. It is a *toovar dahl* that my teammate Milan Doshi learned from his mother. I like to serve it with a spiced basmati rice. Indian recipes use several different dahls (lentils) native to India. Toovar dahl, also known as *arhar*, is a common dish in Indian households. I am grateful to Milan for exposing me to the world of traditional Indian home cooking and eating, whether at a New York temple, his favourite local haunt, or in the school kitchen. He took us on a tour of Indian grocery stores in Queens to show us the array of products, produce, and spices, and helped set me up with my first stainless steel spice tray, called *masala dabba,* which I still use to this day.

TOOVAR DAHL

VEGAN AND GLUTEN FREE

Adapted from Milan Doshi's family recipe

Ingredients

5 tablespoons olive oil

2 cinnamon sticks

7 cloves, ground

1 teaspoon cumin seeds

1 teaspoon brown mustard seeds

12 curry leaves, fresh if possible (optional)

6 large cloves garlic, minced or grated

3 tablespoons grated ginger

2 fresh Thai red chili peppers, seeds removed, small dice, more if you want it hotter

1 large onion, medium dice

½ cup crushed tomatoes

½ teaspoon turmeric

1 ½ tablespoon sea salt, more if needed by taste

2 cups toovar dahl, washed and drained

6 cups curry stock (see recipe below) or vegetable stock

2 tablespoon lemon juice

8 sprigs cilantro, minced for garnish

Directions

- In large pot, heat oil. Once warm, add cinnamon and cloves. After few moments, add cumin seeds and mustard seeds. Once mustard seeds begin to pop, add curry leaves (optional), garlic, grated ginger and Thai chili peppers. Add onion. Once translucent, add crushed tomatoes, turmeric and salt. Allow to cook for five to ten minutes.

- Add toovar dahl and curry stock, bring to boil, and then bring down to medium heat. Allow to cook for thirty to forty minutes on medium heat. Add lemon juice and more salt to taste. Add more stock or water if the soup becomes too thick. Take out the cinnamon sticks before serving.

- Serve over Spiced Basmati Rice (recipe follows) and garnish with cilantro.

Yields six to eight servings

Notes:
The word dahl refers to a bean or lentil that has had the outer husk removed and the remaining lentil split. This ensures a quicker cooking time and a softer, creamier textured when cooked. Toovar dahl, also known as toor dahl or arhar dahl, is one of the most popular lentils in India. A yellow split pea with an earthy taste, it is high in protein and fibre and low in fat.

CURRY STOCK

Ingredients
4 tablespoons olive oil
2 pounds carrots, about 10 carrots, cut into ½ inch pieces
1 pound zucchini, about 4 zucchini, cut into ½ inch pieces
½ pound celery, about 6 celery stalks, cut into ½ inch pieces
1 ½ pounds onions, about 3 onions, cut into ½ inch pieces
1 bunch parsley, chopped
8 garlic cloves, peeled and smashed
10 whole cloves
4 tablespoons coriander seeds
2 tablespoons cumin seeds
1 teaspoon sea salt
16 cups or more water
24 curry leaves (optional)

Directions

- In a medium stockpot, heat oil. Add the cloves, coriander, and cumin seeds and wait until they become fragrant, a minute or two. Add the carrots, zucchini, celery, onions, parsley, garlic, and salt. Cook for fifteen to twenty minutes over medium heat, but do not brown.

- Then add 16 cups of water or more. Cover and bring to a boil. Lower heat and simmer for thirty minutes, uncovered.

- Strain stock through a colander.

Yields about 12 cups

Notes:

Store extra stock in containers or ziplock plastic bags in the freezer for easy access. Mark how many cups are in each so you easily take out what you need for a recipe.

SPICED BASMATI RICE

Ingredients

2 cups basmati rice
1 onion, chopped finely
¼ cup olive oil
2 teaspoons cumin seeds
1 teaspoon fennel seeds
¼ teaspoon turmeric
1 teaspoons ground black pepper
1 cinnamon stick
2 ⅔ cup water
1 teaspoon sea salt

Directions

- Wash rice in several changes of water untll the water is clear. Drain with sieve.

- Heat the oil in a pan over medium heat. When hot, put in the onion. Stir and fry the onion until lightly browned. Add the spices and rice to the pan, cook and stir about thirty seconds until everything is coated with the oil.

- Add the water and salt and bring the rice to a boil. Cover with a lid and turn the heat to simmer for about fifteen to twenty minutes. Remove from heat. Let stand for five to ten minutes before opening. Remove cinnamon stick and fluff rice with fork before serving.

Yields six to eight servings

Notes:

The Hindi word basmati means fragrant, and refers to the nutlike flavor and aroma of this small but long-grained rice. It has been used in India and Pakistan for thousands of years. Ayurvedic philosophy recommends basmati rice because it is pure and easy on the digestive system.

PEELING SHALLOTS

I interned at Candle 79, a fabulous vegan restaurant on the upper east side of Manhattan. Celebrities and foodies love their amazing whole foods vegan philosophy and cuisine.

On October 15, 2006, I wrote a blog entry from New York detailing the kind of work I had to do—peeling shallots until I could barely feel my hands.

I'm just back from Sunday shift at the restaurant. I've survived, but my legs are swollen from standing for over ten hours straight, my fingers burning and sore after a six-hour session with the shallots from hell, cutting the end off each and peeling it carefully. I ended up with over ten quarts of shallots, which may not sound like a lot, especially if you're a pro, but believe me, peeling them was labour intensive. I did one bag and I was thankful it was over. But then they brought out another big bag, and then another big bag. Peeling the shallot skins made my hands very raw.

The work wasn't always easy, but the company was good. Spanish was the kitchen's common language. During prep shifts, the guys would put on lively Spanish music and sing or dance. I was the only *gringo* and woman in the kitchen, and in their broken English they would ask questions like about if I was married, why I wasn't, and if I had children. I thought I would learn culinary terms, but I learned more random Spanish.

Besides the questioning about personal life, they paid no attention to me. The odd time they would glance at me cutting an onion carefully and then throw it out because it was not acceptable to them. Occasionally, in half English and half Spanish, a cook would direct me to get something from the walk-in fridge downstairs. I would often not understand, and they would get angry and gesture to me to get going. I'd have to guess at what to bring back. Cooks are often forced to supervise interns, and I think I was seen as more of a hindrance than help. I did likely provide some comic relief in their day-to-day routines.

These guys would start in professional kitchens from the bottom at a young age and become incredibly quick and productive prep and line cooks. You could see their love for Mexican home cooking, learned from their dearly loved mothers back home. They spoke fondly of these women and hoped to return home one day. I loved their guacamole; they were quite precise in handling avocado and cilantro. Here is the recipe for guacamole that I learned from the Candle 79 cooks, leaving out the critical technical parts and keeping the intention and the love. Serve it with tortilla or pita chips: it's delicious.

GUACAMOLE

VEGAN AND GLUTEN FREE

Ingredients

6 ripe avocados mashed
3-4 tablespoons lime juice (1 lime)
½ bunch cilantro or 2 cups, minced
¼ cup red onion, finely chopped
1 jalapeno pepper deseeded and minced, or 2 Thai red chili peppers deseeded and minced
Sea salt to taste

Directions

◆   *Mix together with mortar and pestle or use a potato masher. Salt to taste.*

Yields two cups

ZA'ATAR PITA CHIPS

VEGAN

Ingredients

Pita
Sea salt
Olive oil
Za'atar mixture (thyme, sesame seeds toasted, ground sumac)

Directions

- *Preheat oven to 350 degrees Fahrenheit.*

- *Cut pita into triangles or other shapes with scissors. Toss with olive oil, salt and Za'atar mixture.*

- *Put on a baking tray with parchment paper in a single layer. Bake for about 7-10 minutes until lightly browned and crisp. Cool.*

POP-UP DINNER

ZenKitchen was founded on a pop-up dinner concept. I worked on the menu for the first pop-up experience with my co-chef Gregg for some time. The dishes I chose were "converters," a term we came up with to describe food that non-vegans would like. I chose familiar dishes. I knew the Zen-Kitchen cuisine would have to exceed diners' expectations and be better than the "regular" or omnivorous versions. Most guests were meat eaters and were skeptical about vegan, whole foods tasting good.

We planned a four-course feast. The opener was *harira*, a Moroccan lentil soup, followed by our Caesar salad with organic baby romaine and mizuna, vegan vinaigrette, and toasted herbed croutons. The main was butternut squash gnocchi with white bean puree, mushroom-ancho cream, and sautéed *Le Coprin* exotic mushrooms. We finished with a Mexican hot chocolate torte, rich with dark chocolate, *crème anglaise,* and blood orange sauce.

When I arrived at the café the afternoon of the dinner, the owner said that the staff had quit and I had no one to serve or wash dishes. Gregg and I were new in the kitchen, but here we were, working out of a place that was crowded with soup pots and had only minimal equipment to prepare and serve a gourmet dinner for thirty-five. We were particularly stressed until an experienced cook and friend, Louis, walked into the kitchen out of the blue and said he thought we could use his help. My friend Rosanna rushed into the café around this time to say that she had major plumbing problems at her house, she hadn't changed, and she needed to go home before the dinner. When she saw the look of distress on my face, she made the decision to help. She said she would be right back. And she was, with her sister Susan in tow. Rosanna was a server and Susan became our dishwasher.

I knew that I wanted this dinner to be special and create community. I started with a moment of gratitude for what we were about to eat from my longtime yoga teacher and friend Kaia. Mindfulness had become a way of life for me, and I wanted to bring it to the food with which we were nourishing our bodies. At the end of the meal, Moe Garahan, the executive director of Just Food, an organization that works for a just and sustainable food system, spoke to these themes. Then the diners had the opportunity to ask me and the other cooks questions about what they had eaten. I knew that this was important. People needed to love the food, to be curious about it, to speak to others at their table and to have a dialogue. The guests soaked this all up as you would delicious juices with crusty vegan bread. The majority of questions and comments focused around the perception that they didn't know vegan food could be this satisfying. I told them that good food is good food.

MOROCCAN RED LENTIL SOUP
VEGAN AND GLUTEN FREE

Ingredients

¼ cup or more olive oil

2 onions, chopped

½ bunch dill, chopped

½ bunch mint, chopped

⅛ cup ginger, peeled and grated

5 garlic cloves, peeled and minced

2 bay leaves

1 tablespoon ground chili pepper (more or less to taste)

1 tablespoon cumin

1 tablespoon smoked paprika

2 sticks celery, chopped finely

2 cups/16 oz. red lentils, washed and drained

10 cups or more vegetable stock (see recipe below) or store-bought stock

1 lemon, juiced

1 28-ounce can whole peeled tomatoes, rough chopped, or crushed tomatoes

Sea salt and freshly ground pepper to taste

Directions

* Heat a large stock pot over medium heat and add the olive oil. Sautee the onions in olive oil until tender but not browned. If the mixture becomes too dry, add a little water or stock.

* Combine the mint and dill with the onions. Add ginger, garlic, bay leaves, ground chili pepper, cumin, smoked paprika, and celery and cook for a few more minutes. Reduce heat and simmer about five to ten minutes.

* Wash the red lentils in cold water until the water becomes clear, and drain. Add lentils and then the stock to the pot. Bring to boil and simmer for twenty to thirty minutes, stirring often.

- Once the lentils are completely cooked, add lemon juice and tomatoes. Let cook five to ten more minutes.

- Remove the bay leaves. Season with salt and pepper.

- If a smoother consistency for the soup is desired, puree half or all of the soup in a blender or with an immersion blender.

Yields ten servings

Notes:
Don't add the lemon juice or tomatoes until you reach the desired consistency for the lentils, as the acid will prevent the lentils from softening further.

VEGETABLE STOCK

Ingredients
16 cups cold water
4 large onions, quartered
10 garlic cloves, whole
3 carrots, thickly sliced
2 celery stalks, coarsely chopped
½ bunch parsley
⅛ cup peppercorns
2 bay leaves
4-inch piece of dashi kombu
24 dried shiitake mushrooms

Directions

- Wash, peel and chop vegetables. Place vegetables in a large stock pot with parsley, bay leaves, peppercorns, kombu, dried mushrooms, and cold water.

- Bring to a boil; then simmer for an hour or more uncovered.

- Strain the stock through a colander. Bring to a boil. Reduce heat and let stock simmer for one to one and a half hours. Remove from the stove and strain with a fine colander.

SCHUG SAUCE
VEGAN AND GLUTEN FREE

Schug sauce is a Middle Eastern hot sauce that is the staple of Israeli cuisine. It originated in Yemeni cuisine and was brought to Israel by Yemenite Jews. You can use it as a condiment for soups, sandwiches, and so on. This sauce is delicious swirled over the Moroccan red lentil soup.

Ingredients

2 serrano or jalapeno chili peppers, deseeded and chopped
12 garlic cloves, roasted with 2 cups extra virgin olive oil
1/2 bunch cilantro, chopped stems and leaves
1 tablespoon ground cumin
3/4 teaspoon ground cardamom
Sea salt and freshly ground black pepper to taste

Directions

- Roast the garlic with oil in a 350 degrees Fahrenheit oven until soft.

- Deseed and chop the serrano or jalapeno chilies. Use gloves or wash hands immediately after touching the chilies!

- Add the chilies, garlic, cilantro, cumin, cardamom, and oil from the garlic in a blender until well combined. Add salt and pepper to taste.

HAPPY ENDINGS

ZenKitchen held the second monthly pop-up dinner at the Helsinki, which had a lounge upstairs, a big nightclub in the basement that would not be in use during our dinner, and a very small kitchen with an electric stove and little counter space. We had planned to set up tables in the nightclub to provide more space for food plating during service. We didn't realize that there were no bright overhead lights—only very dim mood lighting. It was useless to set up in a space where we could barely see each other, never mind the food.

We somehow prepped and served a meal for thirty-six diners in that tiny kitchen. Again, we were grateful to Louis's rescue. By now we had enlisted him to help with the dinners and he came as soon as he could that day after finishing his management job with the public service. It was nothing short of a miracle that we were able to serve the food to many diners at once. We came up against space and equipment restrictions and had limited experience. Later, I came to understand the importance of preparation. I needed to be self-sufficient when I cooked offsite. Problem solving and troubleshooting are standard modus operandi for most chefs. If you can't troubleshoot and you don't have courage, you're in the wrong business.

I love the idea of offering guests an amuse bouche as a way to say—with food—here is something to get your appetite going. I also love the idea of giving guests something at the end of the meal to say thank you for coming, I hope you enjoy this treat, come again. Since most people love chocolate, I decided to end the pop-up meals with a chocolate truffle. It was funny to hear the excited moans and groans from the guests while they were eating their truffles. I started calling the truffles "happy endings," and this stuck. When I opened the restaurant I carried on the tradition of the amuse bouche and happy ending.

CHOCOLATE TRUFFLES

VEGAN AND GLUTEN FREE

Ingredients

½ cup coconut milk

1 teaspoon pure vanilla extract or liqueur of choice

Pinch sea salt

1 cup organic, fair trade semi-sweet chocolate chips

2 tablespoons organic, fair trade cocoa powder

Directions

◆ Combine the coconut milk, vanilla extract, and salt in a small saucepan and bring to a boil, over medium heat. Reduce heat to low and simmer for five minutes.

◆ Remove the coconut mixture from the heat and add the chocolate, stirring with a whisk until the chocolate is melted and the ingredients are thoroughly combined.

◆ Chill the chocolate mixture in the freezer for about one hour, or until it is firm enough to shape into balls. The freezing time will vary widely depending on the freezer. If the mixture becomes too hard, you can always take it out and wait until it softens a bit. If the mixture is still too soft, put it back in the freezer and wait until it is the right consistency to work with.

◆ Place the cocoa powder in a bowl. Using a teaspoon or melon baller, scoop a small amount of chocolate mixture, forming one-inch balls. Roll the balls into the cocoa mixture and place them on a baking sheet lined with parchment paper. Dust your hands with the cocoa mixture and lightly and briefly roll each truffle to further make it into a ball shape, then dredge in cocoa mix-ture to finish. Store the balls in the fridge and take them out before you want to eat them.

Yields about twelve truffles

Notes:

The truffles may be stored in the fridge for one week or in the freezer for up to two months.

CHRISTMAS AT
THE CHELSEA CLUB

There was more or less the same structure for most of the pop-up dinners: a chance for mingling and hors d'oeuvres, a surprise menu with four courses, and the kitchen staff coming out afterward to answer questions about the food. It was heartwarming and satisfying to see the warm, smiling faces around the room and to answer the thoughtful questions. It made me almost cry in joy most of the time and want to hug each person for coming, but I resisted. Now I wish I had let the tears flow. Making them happy made me very happy.

My favourite monthly dinner was always the one before Christmas at The Chelsea Club. There could be no better place in the city to hold a dinner during the festive season. The 1860 mansion was decorated for the season, which made it look like you were a guest at a dinner in a Jane Austen novel. After dinner, I invited the guests to come to the salon for after-dinner drinks and carol singing around the grand piano. I hired someone to play the piano and handed out song sheets. It was like a scene out of *Pride and Prejudice*; the only thing that could have made it better would have been a surprise visit by Colin Firth.

Seriously, seeing the joyous and peaceful faces around the salon was close to perfection for me. I knew at these times more than ever that I was building much more than people coming to monthly dinners. I was building something more lasting. Community.

At one of the holiday-themed dinners, I created a rich adzuki-pumpkin soup and we made crackers in the shape of stars to put on top. That's the kind of detail I loved to create to set the theme and mood for the evening. I chose adzuki bean for its flavour and healthful profile and because it is a symbol of love and happiness in Asian culture. I loved the reaction from guests when they would smile at seeing the beauty of the dish, and I could feel their excitement in anticipation of trying it. It was love and happiness in a bowl, for the maker and receiver. At these times, I would feel the incredible power of food made with love.

ADZUKI-PUMPKIN SOUP
VEGAN AND GLUTEN FREE

Ingredients
6 cups vegetable stock
5 cups cooked adzuki beans
¼ cup brown rice flour
¼ cup olive oil
1 small pumpkin or squash
2 onions, chopped
2 cloves garlic, chopped
2-inch piece ginger, minced
½ teaspoon cumin
¼ teaspoon cinnamon
¼ teaspoon paprika
1 teaspoon fennel seeds
½ teaspoon chili powder
1 14 oz can plum tomatoes, diced, with their juice
2 tablespoons maple syrup
2 tablespoons gluten-free tamari or soy sauce
2 tablespoons sherry vinegar
Sea salt
Garnish
Yoghurt, dairy-free or regular
Pepitas (pumpkin seeds)

Directions
- Preheat oven to 375 degrees Fahrenheit.
- Cut pumpkin or squash in half, remove the seeds and oil it well. Sprinkle with salt and roast cut side down until soft, thirty to forty minutes. Scoop out flesh from skin and set aside.

- *In a pan, heat oil over medium heat and add onion. Caramelize, adding stock as needed to prevent from burning. Add garlic, ginger and spices. Add rice flour and stir in. Add diced tomatoes, with their juice, pumpkin/squash, adzuki beans, maple syrup, tamari/soy sauce and remaining stock.*

- *Bring soup to a boil and then simmer for twenty to thirty minutes. Add sherry vinegar at the end and extra salt if needed. Puree the soup in a blender or with an immersion blender. Garnish with yoghurt and pepitas.*

Yields 16-19 cups

RESTAURANT ADVENTURES

It was one of those frigid November days in Ottawa, and we were waiting in front of a restaurant for the beginning of a scene for our pilot. We walked in and out of potential restaurants, doing the entries and exits over and over. A production crew of eight people followed us closely as we checked out potential restaurant spaces on pilot day. I was really nervous at first, but I knew I needed to be as real as possible on camera and reveal as much as I could about what truly happens when someone decides to open up a restaurant with no experience.

All that waiting was perhaps the most challenging part of being filmed—waiting because they needed to fix the lighting, waiting for a battery pack change, waiting because the director didn't like the set-up, waiting as a location was changed or the contents of a room moved around, waiting because they needed more film, waiting for people to clear in a supermarket or crowd. I now have a lot of compassion for actors and production crews, because they do a fuck of a lot of waiting. There was also the matter of self-exposure. At the beginning I thought I could run from the cameras, but they would find me. And the more I tried to hide personal issues the more they would come out. Moods and glances from different moments in my life were spliced in the editing room to emphasize drama and arguments. I was constantly observed, constantly needing to face emotions. Resisting felt like swimming against the current, and it was exhausting.

Eventually I started seeing the camera as a truth-sayer and ally of sorts. I let go and started floating down the current face up with my feet first. I realized that the crew was there to capture my life in all its drama. We all have our dramas: a car breaks down, a basement floods, keys are lost, someone becomes ill, a child is cranky, you argue with your partner. I signed on for the show, of course, because I wanted promotion for our new restaurant, but I also wanted to be truthful about my life as a chef, entrepreneur, partner, and woman. In being who I was, I allowed others to let down their guards. I also came to see the crew as my dysfunctional family. They were there when I held my last pop-up dinner with the diners I loved. They were there when I found the restaurant, and they captured the spirit of the community that came to support and fund me.

During the filming, I took George to the Japanese Canadian Cultural Centre's Spring Festival, or *Haru Matsuri*, in Toronto. At one point, I lost track of him and my cousin Randy told me he was off dancing to the *taiko* drumming. I ran to the auditorium. Sure enough, there was my dad, dancing in front of an audience of hundreds while the cameras filmed. He called out to me, "Caro, it's a good beat, come dance!" I felt awkward, but I grabbed his hand, keenly aware that I was on camera. The filming made me a better daughter in that moment: I probably wouldn't have started dancing without the pressure of the cameras, and then I would have regretted letting the chance pass. I leaned into that moment, and the cameras actually made that easier for me—I was under scrutiny anyway, so I had nothing to protect.

I shared in the lives of the crew as well. On our director Susan's birthday, I served her a piece of chocolate cake after we wrapped, and she was touched. Often the crew had to film me making and serving food, which must have been hard when they were hungry and tired during long, intense shifts. They said that one of the toughest moments for them was filming me serving the Mexican chocolate cake. Diners said that cake was better than sex, but the crew didn't get to partake. After my filming ended I would sometimes go to their production truck with slabs of chocolate cake drizzled with hot chocolate sauce. I loved seeing their smiles as they saw me approaching with that big plate of delicious cake.

RESTAURANT ADVENTURES

MEXICAN SPICED CHOCOLATE CAKE

VEGAN

Ingredients

2 cups unbleached all-purpose flour

⅞ cup organic, fair trade cocoa powder

2 teaspoons aluminum-free baking powder

1 teaspoon baking soda

½ teaspoon sea salt

2 cups organic soy milk

½ cup canola oil

1 cup maple syrup

½ cup unrefined sugar

2 teaspoons apple cider vinegar

2 teaspoons vanilla extract

Directions

◆ Heat oven to 350 degrees Fahrenheit. Oil a large rectangular baking pan.

◆ Place a wire mesh strainer over a large bowl. Sift the flour, cocoa powder, baking powder, baking soda and salt into the bowl. Stir with a whisk to distribute the ingredients.

◆ In a medium bowl, whisk the soy milk, oil, maple syrup, sugar, vinegar and vanilla thoroughly until well combined. Add the liquid mixture to the dry ingredients and whisk until the batter is smooth.

◆ Fill the pan. Bake until a toothpick inserted in the centre comes out clean, twenty to thirty minutes. Allow to cool.

◆ Glaze with Mexican chocolate sauce (recipe follows).

MEXICAN SPICED CHOCOLATE SAUCE

VEGAN AND GLUTEN FREE

Ingredients

2 cups organic soy milk or other milk

1 dried chipotle pepper

1/8 teaspoon cayenne pepper

Cinnamon stick

Pinch sea salt

2 1/2 cups organic, fair trade semi-sweet chocolate chips

2 teaspoons vanilla extract

Directions

- Bring soy milk, chipotle pepper, cayenne pepper, the cinnamon stick and sea salt to a boil. Reduce heat to simmer for about ten minutes.

- Remove the chipotle pepper and cinnamon stick. Stir in the chocolate and vanilla until just melted.

- If the sauce is too thin, add more chocolate.

BUILD IT, AND THEY WILL COME

Never doubt that a small group of thoughtful, committed citizens
can change the world. Indeed, it is the only thing that ever has.
—Margaret Mead

When I think of phyllo triangles, I think of building community. As I
started cooking professionally for large events I had to think of a dish that
I could make in advance. I didn't have my own kitchen and I relied on The
Chelsea Club's schedule for the pop-up dinners. Phyllo triangles were the
perfect solution: they could be made in advance, frozen, and then heated up
before an event. The downside was that they are laborious to make. At the
beginning of my career as a chef, I did many events for little or no money
in order to promote ZenKitchen. I had no money for labour so I would call
in friends and friends of friends to help. We listened to music and made the
phyllo triangles for hours, talking and laughing.

I was realizing that we might not have the money to open up and maintain
a restaurant. To be honest, had the cameras not been on us for *The Restaurant
Adventures*, we may have given up. The strongest force encouraging us onward
was the monthly dinner community. Our regular diners were enthusiastic for
us to start a restaurant and many came to us to ask how they could help. Their
support was touching, but what we really needed was cash flow.

One day, an idea struck. In the community-supported agriculture model, or CSA, supporters pay farms in advance for produce they later receive during the growing season. Could it be used to start up a restaurant? Perhaps an advance gift certificate program would work: I could host a special event for guests where they would see the space, hear about plans for the renovation, and have the opportunity to buy these gift certificates or "stakes." I could also have guests vote on their favourite pop-up dishes, which would become the basis for the restaurant's menu. We held the event, all the while being filmed. I had to limit the number of people we invited to the open house fundraiser because the restaurant had a fairly small capacity. In a few hours, we had raised over $20,000.

Zen philosophy believes that when we mindfully dwell in the present moment, we completely dissolve into whatever activity manifests. We *become* the activity. Some call this "flow." I learned much about flow from the experience of fundraising for ZenKitchen. Instead of getting stuck in details and sabotaging ourselves, we managed to keep the feeling of flow and let that guide the process.

This recipe for phyllo triangles will always remind me of the hands that built ZenKitchen. The love and support for the restaurant was always incredible. I created my food with much love and care, and those who could feel that love wanted to return it. Customers referred others, sent me notes of appreciation and thanks, offered tips, and ultimately raised the capital that enabled us to open. Of course, phyllo pastry is only the casing for the dish. I've used many fillings through the years, but my customers' favourite was always pesto and tofu cheese. This recipe is for them.

PHYLLO TRIANGLES

PESTO, CHEESE, AND SUNDRIED TOMATO FILLING

VEGAN

Ingredients

1 package of frozen phyllo dough, thawed overnight

1 cup extra virgin olive oil, for brushing phyllo

Pesto

2 cups basil leaves

2 cups kale leaves, chopped

2 garlic cloves, sliced

¼ cup pepitas (pumpkin seeds)

Pinch sea salt

1 cup extra virgin olive oil

Tofu Cheese

1 package of extra firm tofu, not silken, washed and drained

1 tablespoon tahini

1 teaspoon nutritional yeast

½ teaspoon lemon zest

Sundried Tomatoes

2 cups sundried tomatoes, soaked in 2 cups extra virgin olive oil overnight or for 24 hours

Sea salt

Directions

- Soak sundried tomatoes in oil overnight or for 24 hours. Drain. You can then keep the oil for many purposes, such as drizzling on pizza or pasta.

- Take the phyllo dough out of the freezer and let thaw in the refrigerator overnight or for at least twenty-four hours. For the last hour, take out of the fridge.

- Preheat oven to 350 degrees Fahrenheit.

- Assemble the tofu cheese. Blanch the tofu in hot water for a few minutes and drain well. Crumble it in a food processor, or use your hands. Add the tahini, nutritional yeast, and lemon zest. Process in the food processor, or use your hands until well combined. Add sea salt to taste.

- Make the pesto. Add the basil, kale, garlic, pepitas, and sea salt to a blender or food processor and process to a paste. Drizzle in the olive oil. If you need to thin the pesto, add more oil or water.

- Chop the sundried tomatoes. Combine them with the pesto and cheese. Add two tablespoons of the oil from soaking the tomatoes and sea salt to taste.

- To make the triangles, first unroll the phyllo and lay a slightly damp dish towel on top of it to keep it moist. You must make sure that the phyllo is covered at all times as you work with it, as it dries out quickly. Peel off the piece you are using and cover the remaining stack as you work with that piece.

- Arrange one sheet of phyllo on a large cutting board. Dip the pastry brush in the oil and lightly brush the entire surface. Do this two more times, brushing the pastry between layers with oil.

- Cut the phyllo sheet into six long pieces.

- Place about one tablespoon of filling at one end of the strip. Fold up from the corner into a triangle and then continue folding. Transfer the triangle to a parchment-covered baking sheet. Repeat with the remaining phyllo and filling. Brush the tops of the phyllo with oil.

- Bake for about twenty to twenty-five minutes, or until the triangles are lightly browned.

Yields six dozen

BUILD IT, AND THEY WILL COME

Notes:

You can freeze the triangles before baking. Keep them on the parchment on the baking sheet and freeze overnight, or for at least twenty-four hours, until hardened. Transfer to a plastic bag or container. Cook from frozen in a 350 degrees F oven for about thirty to forty minutes, until lightly browned.

LISTEN FOR THE BEAT
AND DANCE TO IT

Before the restaurant opened, and on camera, George collapsed and had to go to the hospital with a heart condition. This shocked me: my father had been very healthy all his life, always had more energy than me, walked for hours each day, and loved being independent. I was suddenly scared that he could die. At eighty-three, he announced that he was getting a bit sore from working all day gardening. He never had complained before.

I began to visit him once a month, like clockwork. I always took him on an excursion. He loved going on the ferry to Centre Island. We went to the house where I was born. Often we went to malls to walk, and anytime I would stop to look at something, he was impatient and fidgeted like a two-year-old. I thought I was doing these monthly visits for my dad, but our visits also nourished me. We ate great food and explored Toronto, free and open as children. I didn't give myself permission to do these kinds of things in my daily life at home.

Going on year two at the restaurant I was overwhelmed. I needed time out from a life that seemed relentless and exhausting. Meanwhile, my dad was trying to fill his days, the hours and minutes dragging on. One day while driving in the car, my dad kept looking at the big face on his watch and telling me the time every five minutes. I got annoyed and told him to stop. He said, "The days are long and boring when you don't have anything to do, and time goes so fast with you. The day is almost over!" I could feel my heart sink in compassion for him. I felt in my heart how most of our adult lives are spent running. When we are much older and all the work and responsibilities are behind us, we regret, as the Buddhist teacher and activist Michael Stone put it, "running to our deaths."

"You just have to listen for the beat and dance to it," George used to say. He loved to dance and laugh. Towards the end of his life, though, what my dad loved most of all was sharing a meal with me when we had our monthly visits. In the morning, he would sometimes wait for more than an hour in the living room, coat and cap on, ready to leave for a breakfast date. Anytime he heard a stirring in my bedroom he would peak in and ask: "Ready for breakfast?"

At the restaurant, he greeted the server and any person who looked his way, saying, "Hi, I'm George" with a big smile. He tried to shake hands or wave a hello. When we were leaving, no matter how busy the server was, he would wait for her—most often women do breakfast service, in my experience—shake her hand again, and thank her profusely.

What my dad liked to enjoy for breakfast, next to coffee, was blueberry pancakes. In honour of my dad, this recipe is for ZenKitchen blueberry pancakes. They are vegan and gluten-free.

BLUEBERRY PANCAKES

VEGAN AND GLUTEN FREE

Ingredients

4 ounces silken tofu

2 cups organic soy milk

3 tablespoons maple syrup

1 teaspoon vanilla extract

1 tablespoon olive oil

2 cups all-purpose flour, gluten-free

½ teaspoon sea salt

1 tablespoon aluminum-free baking powder

1 cup frozen blueberries

½ teaspoon grated lemon zest

Grapeseed or olive oil for the skillet

Directions

♦ Puree the tofu, milk, maple syrup, vanilla and oil in a blender until smooth. Pour into a large bowl. Sift the flour with the salt and baking powder. Mix into liquid mixture with a whisk, using light strokes just enough to combine and leaving it lumpy. Add in frozen blueberries and lemon zest to combine.

♦ Heat a skillet on medium-high heat. Put in oil and twirl around. Turn heat to medium and pour about one-quarter cup for each pancake. Cook on one side until the top bubbles. Flip over and cook the other side for half the time.

Yields twelve pancakes

BLACK BEAN IN JULY

We called the line a "clam bake" in ZenKitchen's early days, when we were all women. We had a lot of fun in those days, and loved to sing while we worked. One of our favourite ways to lighten the kitchen, next to finding strange-looking vegetables, was altering words to well-known songs and sing them over and over, often to the annoyed glares of the front of house staff. One of the most popular dishes on our menu at the time was black bean dip with guacamole. I replaced the words to "Black Day in July" by Gordon Lightfoot to "black bean in July." Apologies to Gordon, but that song provided us with endless amusement. We were like kids, finding the strangest things to keep us amused while doing repetitive tasks and working in the confines of a small, hot space.

I didn't rise up through the ranks like other chefs I know, putting in grueling hours under sadistic chefs. I didn't want to do that; and besides, I came into cooking later in life, so I didn't have the time and patience for any shit. Perhaps it's also because I chose to focus on gourmet vegan cuisine, while the traditional chef cooks meat, fish, and their byproducts. I was nervous when I first started running the kitchen. Some male cooks, particularly sous chefs, said I wasn't a "real" chef; I was too nice, too soft, too collaborative. What they were really saying is that I wasn't the typical dominant male Chef, French style. My "feminine" traits were seen as weaknesses. They told me in their interviews that they hated working in those archaic systems, and that they looked forward to my fresh, collaborative approach. But these were the very things they would end up complaining about. It was like being in a bad relationship.

I thought bringing Zen to the restaurant, and in particular to the kitchen, would be easy. I was wrong. We did have a collaborative approach with the kitchen staff for the monthly pop-up dinners and that was fun, even when we had to burn the midnight oil, prepping like crazy. At ZenKitchen, we started with a good balance of young women in the kitchen. For the most part, we shared mutual respect and appreciation. I kept a Buddha in the kitchen as reminder to stay calm and peaceful. The staff gave him offerings and I like to think he was singing along with us.

This black bean recipe reminds me of those fun "black bean in July" days. Black bean dip was a popular dish on the ZenKitchen menu, served with guacamole, sour cream, hot sauce, salsa, and tortilla chips, all made from scratch. What I loved most about the dish is that it was often served as a tapas sharing plate. I believe that people love sharing food alongside their experiences. I love the old Italian saying *a tavola non s'invecchia*, which means, at the table, one does not grow old. For me, that phrase speaks to the importance of eating together, savouring food with family and friends. Time stands still when we share food.

BLACK BEAN DIP
VEGAN AND GLUTEN FREE

Ingredients

2 cups cooked black beans, rinsed and drained

¼ cup tahini

1 teaspoon cumin

1 teaspoon chili powder

2 tablespoons tomato paste

1 tablespoon agave

1 tablespoon balsamic vinegar

1 tablespoon extra-virgin olive oil

¾ cup warm water or more

1 cup cilantro, chopped

¼ cup lime juice

Sea salt and freshly ground pepper

Garnish

Green onion, sliced thinly on a diagonal

Plum tomato, deseeded, small dice

Cilantro, chopped

Directions

- Combine the black beans, tahini, cumin, chili powder, tomato paste, agave, balsamic vinegar and oil in a blender or food processor. Add the warm water gradually. If the mixture is too thick, add more warm water.

- Transfer to a bowl and fold in cilantro and lime juice. Add salt and pepper to taste.

- Transfer to a serving dish and place the garnish on top.

Yields 3 cups

KIMCHI FIGHTING

I love kimchi, especially the old-fashioned way of using salt brine on the cabbage and pressing it to bring out its slightly fermented, sour taste. I wanted to include kimchi as part of the menu at ZenKitchen, not only because I loved it, but because I knew it was good for people, the fermentation process producing natural probiotics. This was my philosophy: feeding people good food that is good for them. I never imagined how much the staff, especially the kitchen staff, would love the kimchi. At the end of the night the cooks would often eat a bowl of kimchi and rice. I'd sing "everybody was kimchi fighting" to the tune of "Kung Fu Fighting."

I used kimchi in a number of dishes—the Zen tapas plate, a customer favourite that featured mostly Asian-inspired offerings, and on the raw burrito plate. Kimchi takes some time to ferment, so there was always a large batch being used, while another, even larger batch was fermented. At one point, kimchi got too popular with my staff. I had to limit how much they were eating so that I had enough for customers.

Here is that recipe for you to try. You may want to sing "Kimchi Fighting" as you're eating it, because eating while laughing is good medicine for the soul.

KIMCHI
VEGAN AND GLUTEN FREE

Kimchi is a fermented cabbage pickle that originates in Korea. Containing a wealth of antioxidants and being a natural probiotic, it has a number health benefits, in particular for the digestive system. Made in a similar way to sauerkraut, you can adjust the spiciness to your liking.

Ingredients
2 pounds Napa cabbage, coarsely chopped
12 red radishes, sliced thin
4 carrots, cut into thin matchsticks
4 onions, minced
10 cloves garlic, minced
6-8 red chilies, minced (please wear rubber gloves and protect your eyes!)
⅓ cup grated ginger
½ cup coarse salt
¼ cup Korean red chili powder (amount depends on the heat you would like)
Filtered water

Directions
* Make a brine of eight cups water and eight tablespoons coarse salt. Mix the vegetables, garlic, chilies, ginger and Korean chili powder in a clean bucket or large pot. Pour the brine over the vegetables. Weigh the vegetables down with a heavy plate so they are submerged in brine. Leave a few hours or overnight is best.

* Drain the vegetables, reserving the brine. Press the vegetables with the heavy plate until the liquid (which will appear while pressing) rises above the plate. Add a little brine if required.

* Weigh the plate down with a sealed bag of the brine or other heavy object. Cover the pot or container with cheesecloth and leave it for a week or so, checking each

day that the vegetables are submerged. When the kimchi tastes the way you like it, transfer it to jars and refrigerate. It will keep for months in the refrigerator.

GOLD MEDAL PLATES

The biggest confirmation I was doing something right as a chef was receiving a letter inviting me to the prestigious Gold Medal Plates, or GMP. The GMP dinner features a city's top eight or ten chefs, as selected by the GMP committee, to compete in raising funds for Canada's Olympic athletes. I was the first female chef invited to the Ottawa competition, and the first vegan chef invited in the history of the competition in Canada. I wasn't too confident at first. Who was I to win, a newcomer to the restaurant scene, making vegan food that did not have the ingredients that, traditionally, chefs use to win over the judges—*foie gras*, bacon, duck fat?

But on the other hand, who was I not to? People loved my creations.

I am often asked how I prepared for the GMP. When a seed is planted in my head, like the GMP, then my creative soul awakens. I listen and trust my intuition. In cooking and in life, there are clues and signs of what direction I am to go in. And if I don't shut down or criticize my out-of-the-box nature, I'm capable of great creativity. I always keep a book in which to record ideas and thoughts, and take photos of images that resonate with me on some level. I might see swatches of fabric that I love together, or the position of items in a display window that are fascinating, or something in nature that is too beautiful not to capture. I clip out pictures from magazines. I look through cookbooks and culinary magazines. When I go out to restaurants, I take photographs of the food so that I remember its presentation, the way that chef has complemented or contrasted components or highlighted certain ingredients.

Planning my GMP dish, I had a vision of a Zen garden. The components changed over time as my crew and I tested each one. In the end, what I presented included a base of polenta cake with a thin layer of red pepper aspic on top. An exotic Le Coprin mushroom ragout surrounded the polenta like a pond, and a smoked yuba roll filled with macadamia nut cheese sat on top like an offering. Dots of pasilla chili sauce, meant to resemble pebbles, decorated the plate. We chose an Angels Gate Winery 2008 Archangel sparkling rose for the wine pairing.

My sous-chef Jonathan encouraged me to win the silver medal. This was ideal, he said; it would be a lot of work, money, and stress to win the gold and go further into competition on the west coast. The silver was perfect, he explained, because we would get the recognition but not have to make any more effort. I told him I would try, as if you could will these things to happen. I started imagining winning silver.

Before the competition, we were running to get ready at Canada's National Arts Centre for a six o'clock start. It wasn't easy to be in a foreign kitchen, working on several levels with one fob key, and nine other anxious teams doing the same. Just before six, we got our fifteen-minute warning from the judges via one of my staff, who had spent five of the fifteen minutes in a panic trying to find where we were. We had been selected to go first. When I finally presented the food, I told the judges that the plate was inspired by a Zen garden and spoke to them about the components. They smiled politely, thanked me, and I left. At one point during the competition the head judge came to ask us about ingredients I had listed in the description of the dish, because most of the judges had never heard of them.

In announcing the winner, the head judge said that they'd had a long discussion about who would take first. The silver winner was apparently just one vote away from first place. As I stood there listening to him, I had this sudden realization that he was going to call my name for the silver. When he did, I was shocked. I ran to the podium in excitement to receive my medal.

I had hoped for the win, but so had the other very talented chefs in the room. This was one of the happiest moments of my life. I felt I won a battle against people thinking vegan food is inferior, granola, or not sophisticated. I now considered myself a professional, accomplished chef.

This recipe for exotic mushroom ragout and polenta is a pared-down, home cook's version of the winning plate, made more appropriate for preparing in your own kitchen.

EXOTIC MUSHROOM
WHITE BEAN RAGOUT WITH POLENTA

VEGAN AND GLUTEN FREE

Ingredients

¼ cup olive oil

2 onions, sliced

2 garlic cloves, minced

1 teaspoon dried thyme

½ teaspoon chili flakes

¼ cup brown rice flour

1 pound, or 4-6 cups, of assorted fresh mushrooms such as cremini, button, oyster

1 cup tomato sauce

1 cup dried mushrooms rehydrated in 2 cups boiling water for 30 minutes and chopped

1 ½ cups stock created while rehydrating the mushrooms

1 cup red wine

1 14 oz. can cannellini or other beans, drained and rinsed

1 tablespoon agave

1 tablespoon gluten-free tamari or soy sauce

Sea salt and freshly ground pepper

¼ cup chopped parsley

Directions

* Sauté onions for about twenty minutes until they begin to caramelize. If the onions become too dry, add mushroom stock a little at a time.

* Add garlic, thyme and chili flakes. Deglaze with a little mushroom stock.

* Add rice flour and stir for a few minutes. Add chopped fresh mushrooms, tomato sauce, rehydrated mushrooms pieces and red wine. Add remaining stock.

* Simmer for twenty to thirty minutes. Add beans, agave, and tamari/soy sauce. Season with salt and pepper to taste.

* Turn off heat and sprinkle chopped parsley on top. Serve over polenta.

GOLD MEDAL PLATES

POLENTA

VEGAN AND GLUTEN FREE

Adapted from Essentials of Classic Italian Cooking by Marcella Hazan

Ingredients
1 ⅔ cups coarse-grained yellow cornmeal

7 cups water

2 teaspoons salt

Directions
◆ Bring water to boil in a large pot. Add the salt, keeping the water boiling at medium-high heat, and then add the cornmeal in a very thin stream. The entire time you are adding the cornmeal, stir it with a whisk and make sure the water is always boiling.

◆ When you have put in all the cornmeal, begin to stir with a wooden spoon, stirring continuously, bringing the mixture up from the bottom and loosening it from the sides of the pot. Reduce the heat to medium-low so that the mixture simmers rather than boils.

◆ Continue to stir for forty to forty-five minutes. The cornmeal becomes polenta when it forms a mass that starts pulling away from the sides of the pot. If you would like to eat the polenta soft and hot, serve it at once, but leftover polenta is delicious! Smooth the polenta on a flat board to the thickness of about three inches and let it become completely cold and firm, which takes a few hours to overnight. You can then slice and grill, bake, or fry it.

Notes:
The stirring time of forty to forty-five minutes is not an error. I checked with several Italian friends and they had lots of polenta stories. They said they used to get in trouble from their moms when walking away from the pot! You can buy polenta that requires less cooking time and is almost as good. I'm not a fan of the ready-made sausage-shaped polenta rolls.

MOM'S SPARE RIBS

I learned a lot from my mom in the kitchen from the time I was very young, though she had high standards and was not very patient with the stubby, clumsy fingers of a child. Food, cooking and restaurants were our shared language.

I recall the last conversation I had with my mother, before she had her third and final stroke at sixty. She was fairly housebound because of her strokes and lonely. She would call me in Ottawa from Toronto just to chat. These calls could last for hours; I'd chat with her on my cordless telephone and do chores while keeping her company. During that final call, I was in my Ottawa apartment preparing a dinner for friends. I tried to get her off of the line because I was in a rush to get ready for this dinner, but as usual she didn't want to go and I didn't have the heart to hang up, so we continued the conversation as I went through my preparations. I had decided to make her spare ribs, but she didn't have a recipe. She just used her instincts. She had given me basic directions for the ribs the night before and then she talked me through the rest of the steps while we were on the phone.

She wasn't linear about it and I found myself getting frustrated. What happened when? What did I do after this step was completed? She didn't tell me how to make the ribs in order. It was not only my mother's cooking but also her life that was not linear. I see now that I carried on this non-linear approach. I spent most of my life resisting my parents, wanting to be different than them, better, smarter, more educated, more "Canadian."

In the end, I realize I am very much like them. While I was busy trying to be what they are not, I didn't understand that the traits that they had passed on to me since I was a child couldn't be erased. From them, I learned to be kind and generous, to give, work hard and be humble. I learned that nothing is beneath us, and to appreciate what you have and not be wasteful.

My mother was incredibly smart, creative and generous, and if I got that from her, I am grateful. We can't choose what we get from our parents, but we can choose what to use or not.

My mother never used a recipe to cook Japanese food. It was in her head and heart. She would often make things from what was available in the kitchen, and I would watch in fascination as she would add a dash of this, a sprinkle of that, tasting along the way until the *aji* (taste) was exactly to her liking. She wasted nothing; there was always a use for something, or a second use. I'm definitely her daughter: from the time I was a teenager I would visit my friend's houses and rummage around in their fridge and cupboards to cook up something from what they had on hand. When I went camping, I would go through the food supplies in coolers to figure out what I could make over the campfire. I was and am always resourceful, much like my mother. It would frustrate me when my cooks would use what they wanted from a vegetable and throw the rest away because they couldn't be bothered to wrap it up, put it in the stock bin—or better yet, think of a use for it, like an amuse bouche.

My mother passed on her recipe for spare ribs and then collapsed shortly afterwards from the stroke that induced a lasting coma. You never know what the last memory will be with someone. She never wrote down her recipes and this is the only written one we found after she died. She would be happy to know it is still feeding others.

MOM'S SPARE RIBS

MOM'S SPARE RIBS

GLUTEN FREE

Ingredients

2-3 pounds pork spare ribs

1 tablespoon sea salt

¼ cup gluten-free tamari or soy sauce

¼ cup cooking sake

½ cup unrefined brown sugar

1 tablespoon grated ginger

1 14 ounce can pineapple chunks and juice

1 cup potato starch

1 tablespoon roasted sesame seeds

About 4 cups of cooking oil

Directions

- Cut ribs into bite-size pieces. Put meat pieces in a large pot, cover with water and add the salt. Bring to boil and then simmer for about forty-five minutes. Skim the foam as it rises with a slotted spoon.

- In a bowl, mix together the tamari/soy sauce, sake, ginger and brown sugar. Add the pineapple chunks and juice.

- Prepare a deep fryer: put oil in big pot and heat until it reaches 350 degrees Fahrenheit (use a cooking thermometer to measure the temperature of the oil).

- Roll each piece of meat in potato starch, shaking off any excess.

- Fry meat in batches until they become a darker brown, about five to ten minutes for each batch. Be careful to not overcrowd the ribs as you are frying them.

- Place ribs in a casserole dish. Mix the tamari/soy sauce mixture with the ribs.

- Bake the ribs in 350 degrees Fahrenheit oven until the mixture thickens, about twenty to thirty minutes. Serve sprinkled with sesame seeds.

Notes:

For a vegan version of this recipe, you can replace the spare ribs with two packages or blocks of firm tofu cut into one-inch cubes. You don't need to boil the tofu as you would the spareribs.

COMFORT FOOD FOR GEORGE

On Thanksgiving Day in 2012, my sister called to say that she was at the hospital with dad because he had been complaining of shortness of breath. When I arrived in Toronto he was back at home in bed and couldn't move. I walked into his bedroom, and he told me, "You're looking really good, Caro."

I replied, "You're not, dad," and laughed with him. He was unable to move and suffering. I did everything I could do to help him, to make him feel better, to be with him. I gave him medication and fed him, although he had little appetite.

I returned to Ottawa and to the restaurant. Soon after I arrived home I got a call from my sister that dad was back in the hospital. I took a train back to Toronto to see him. This became a regular occurrence, to the point that I was often travelling twice a week from Ottawa to Toronto. On one visit, I went to visit dad and brought him a coffee and blueberry muffin, his favourite. He seemed exhausted and weak, but in better spirits as he drank coffee. He asked me his usual three questions. Did I have enough money? Did I need something to eat? How was the weather? I hugged him as I said good-bye, and he waved like he loved to do, trying to smile. It broke my heart to leave him in the hospital alone and the tears that I had held back came flooding in as I drove to the train station.

Soon after, during dinner service at the restaurant, I got another call from my sister. She said that dad had taken a turn and I needed to come as soon as possible. I took the overnight bus, which felt like I was in a dark, enclosed tomb for five hours. I was a captive being transported by the enemy to a secret destination. My sister picked me around five in the morning and took me to the hospital.

My dad was breathing through tubes. He needed morphine to help him sleep. He looked so old and fragile, a fragment of the man I knew. He tried to open his eyes and acknowledge me, to move his head forward from the pillow and nod, but he quickly collapsed back again. I held his withered, wrinkly hand tightly in mine, and told him over and over again how much I loved him, thanking him for what he had brought into my life. And then, sometime between my leaving his side in the early evening and around midnight, he died. I often hear that people die just as a loved one leaves their side, as if they want to spare the beloved seeing their death—a last act of love.

At George's service, I gave a eulogy. I asked for the courage to speak from my heart and make it through. I felt that my dad was there with me in the room, happy to hear what I was saying and trying to get me to laugh. That was always his way, even during serious situations like funerals. Some people would give him the same look they give to children who are being noisy, but he didn't care. He was the eternal child. When people asked him his age, he offered a really high or really low number and watched their expression for a few seconds, waiting for them to laugh.

Although it was tremendously painful, being with my dad near the end woke me up to what was really important in life. The only thing that mattered during that period was him—caring for him and being there for him. And after he died, I realized I was exhausted, spent, sad and in need of change. His death gave me the courage and determination to make that change happen. I went back home after the funeral and told Dave that I wanted to leave our relationship and ZenKitchen as well. We had been skirting around our issues for a while without resolution and we both felt unhappy.

From there, the ZenKitchen era came to a quick end. I cleaned up and staged the house; it went on sale just before Christmas in 2012. We told the staff in January that we had separated and that I would be taking a sabbatical

COMFORT FOOD FOR GEORGE

starting in February to write a book and travel. The agreement for the transfer of the restaurant to Dave was finally signed in April, and this was announced to staff and media. I walked away from everything that I had created: a restaurant I'd owned for four years, and a pop-up I'd envisioned and run for two more.

What became apparent after the coming years of rest, travel and healing, however, was that I was making a journey home, towards myself. I had started the ZenKitchen journey years before, and its impact on the community was beyond my wildest imagination. Now I was starting fresh again, not knowing what I'd do with my cooking or where I'd end up next. All I knew is that courage to face and tell the truth would again support me in finding my way.

In honour of George, I offer a recipe for Japanese curry—one of his favourite dishes. You may be surprised that Japanese home cuisine has curry in its repertoire. The British introduced curry to Japan during the *Meiji* era (1868–1912), when India was under their administration. The dish became popular in Japan and available for purchase in supermarkets; it's now so loved that Japan can claim it as a national dish. Japanese curry is influenced by Indian-style curry but is milder and sweeter. Some of this sweetness comes from fruits like bananas or apples.

Often the Japanese use a packaged curry *roux* as a starter. A roux is flour cooked in equal parts fat and used as a thickener. Using prepackaged curry roux and mixing it with spices makes preparing a curry easy and quick. I've come up with a recipe for from-scratch curry in which you can make your own spice mix. Because this adds another step, I suggest making a large batch to keep on hand. Instead of rice, you can also serve the curry with noodles, bread or potatoes.

In Japan, curry is a very popular dish among children.

JAPANESE-INSPIRED CURRY
VEGAN AND GLUTEN FREE

Ingredients
1 cauliflower, cut into small florets
1 squash (kabocha or other), diced medium
2 onions, thinly sliced
1 small piece of ginger, peeled and grated
¼ cup garam masala
⅛ cup brown rice flour
½ cup crushed tomatoes
2 carrots, cut into half moons
1 apple peeled, cored, and cut into thin slices
1 banana, cut into thin slices
6 cups stock or more
1 24 oz. package of tempeh, coarsely grated
4 cups coconut milk
Sea salt and freshly ground pepper to taste
Olive oil

Directions
- Heat oven to 400 degrees Fahrenheit.

- Toss cauliflower and squash in oil and bake for twenty to thirty minutes or until tender. If you use a squash like kabocha, you can keep the skin on.

- Heat oil in a large saucepan over medium heat. Sauté the onions until they are golden brown and caramelized, around fifteen to twenty minutes.

- Add the ginger, stirring with the onions. Add the garam masala, combining with the other ingredients. Add the rice flour and again combine. Stir in the tomatoes. Add the carrots, apple, banana, and grated tempeh.

- Cover with the stock and bring to boil.

- Simmer for about twenty to thirty minutes, stirring occasionally, until the vegetables are tender and the apple and banana slices have dissolved.

- Add roasted vegetables and coconut milk and simmer for about five to ten minutes. Season with sea salt and freshly ground pepper.

- Serve with Japanese rice (recipe follows).

STOVETOP JAPANESE RICE

Ingredients
1 cup Japanese short-grain rice (not sweet rice)
1 cup plus 2 tablespoons water

Directions
- Measure out the rice into a pot. Fill the pot with enough cold water to cover the rice.

- Gently stir and mix the rice with your hand. Pour the water away when it becomes cloudy and keep the rice in the bowl with your hand. Repeat at least six times or more until the water becomes clear.

- Pour the rice into a sieve and let the excess water drain away. Transfer the rice back to the pot.

- Add the water to your pot.

- Put the pot on the stove at maximum heat until the water boils. Once the water boils, turn down the heat to minimum and let the rice simmer for about fifteen to twenty minutes.

- *Once the rice has simmered, remove the pot from the stove and leave the rice to steam covered for a further ten to fifteen minutes.*

Yields two cups cooked rice

Notes:
- *One cup of dry rice will make about two cups of cooked rice.*

- *Washing the rice is essential to removing as much surface starch as possible and ensures that the cooked rice is not too sticky. If you have time, let the rice sit in the water for at least twenty to thirty minutes before cooking, which will allow the grains to absorb water and cook more evenly. If you are short on time, this soaking can be skipped.*

- *Letting the rice sit covered once finished is essential for getting the correct texture. The finished rice should be glossy and tender but not too sticky. Avoid lifting the lid while the rice is cooking or the steam will escape.*

AFTERWARD

BAKING BREAD WITH GRANDMA ISHII

Know your garden.
It is time to speak your Truth.
Create your community.
Be good to each other.
And do not look outside yourself for the leader.

—Hopi Elder

When my grandmother Ishii was in the Slocan internment camp in Lemon Creek, Alberta, she used to go from shack to shack, asking for extra flour, and then would make bread for everyone to share. That says a lot about our family. That story touches my heart deeply. Despite all the challenges our family has faced collectively and individually, we always think of other people. I am no different. I am a child of this upbringing and it has been passed on much like the bread my grandmother shared in the camp. I would bet that my grandmother ate little or none of the bread she made and was happy about that. I would be.

I have spent my whole life trying not to be who I am: kind, generous, always thinking of other people. People warned that others would take advantage, hurt me, disappoint me. Those who love me dearly said that I needed to protect myself, let only those who are good for me into my space, think of myself first. But if there is a problem with showing love and compassion to others, I'd like to know what that is. Now, after much searching, I realize that we can only find the invisible boundary between others and ourselves by being more compassionate and loving, not less. We need to move without fear towards the line, and sometimes cross it, in order to feel the stab in the heart that tells us to pause. If we always live below the line, we cannot give. In relationships or not, I've sometimes felt that deep well of loneliness, aloneness, that pops up when you least expect it. I've come to realize that the most important thing we can do as a community of human beings is take the time to show others that we care. What is more important than that? Are we too busy to do it? Ultimately, I am on the side of love and compassion. I sincerely hope that in my lifetime there will be a pull away from fear and scarcity.

I felt compelled by love to write this book and I hope that you feel nourished and inspired to do what you love, too. The heart doesn't lie; it is leading the way for us. And what could be a better way to celebrate than through food made with love?

ACKNOWLEDGEMENTS

I believe that the sum is greater than its parts. This was proven in large measure in creating ZenKitchen, my first labour of love, and the book that you are holding in your hands, my second.

I would like to thank my dear friend Barb Brook, who exemplifies love in action. She held the light on the path so I could see my way; she was my cheerleader when I struggled to begin and as I continued to write. When I was impatient to get the book into the world, she led me with her expert project management and coaching skills and with her friendship. I am so grateful for her support—I feel we created this book together.

My editor Laura McGavin is another blessing in my life. She took my words and made my voice stronger and clearer. I call her "the midwife of babies and books." She is actually a birth doula, as well as being an accomplished editor. She took my book under her loving care and editorial expertise, and helped me birth something we both adore.

Countless people helped me in realizing this book, people that Barb called "Team Caroline," offering physical, emotional and spiritual support for this project. I am humbled by and grateful for them.

- Timothy Jones, a gifted graphic designer, was able to translate my book into his world of art and design, which resulted in its beautiful cover design. He worked with the talented and enthusiastic Cäcilia Winand on the book's design and layout.

- Chris Childs, a fabulous editor, proofread the final manuscript.

- Shawn Murphy, a seasoned communications expert, wrote my bio for the book and provided communications support.

- Paul Jones used his photography skills to transition from capturing birds in flight to chefs in flight! And Krishna Mercer, with her partner Magi Reyes, and

Jill Pyle contributed photos they captured of ZenKitchen food and moments, and Yuki Itoh of chef school in New York City.

- Mountain Road Productions, in particular Tim Alp and Margie Robitaille, also contributed photos taken while filming *The Restaurant Adventures of Caroline and Dave*.

- My cousin Randy Okihiro and his wife Cris offered up family photos and recipes, along with encouraging words and good food.

- Family and friends helped me with testing the recipes for the book, including my niece Erin O'Connor, Michael Gazier, Scott Adams and Rossana Rebeccani.

- Several friends and family members provided love and shelter for my possessions and me so that I could comfortably finish the book. Angela Regnier, Cressida Firth, David Irish, Deborah Rolls, Kristen Smith, Kurt Baumgartner and Fran Wright, Marcia and Don O'Connor, Rell DeShaw, Susan Plastino, Yuki Itoh and Rudi Hermawan—thank you.

- Catherine and Allan Green, Judith Brooks and Kaia Nightingale offered emotional and spiritual support to help lift my dreams off the ground.

Many ZenKitchen staff, too numerous to name, helped bring my creations to life by cooking and serving them with care, day after day. Thank you! In the pop-up dinner days, Gregg Lewis, Louis Radakir and Pamela Hart came to the rescue in the kitchen. In particular, Dave Loan—my ex-partner and the co-founder of ZenKitchen—believed in my dream of becoming a chef. I know he loved ZenKitchen as much as I did.

I am still deeply touched and inspired by the community that rallied around ZenKitchen, attending pop-up dinners, providing funds through the Community Support Restaurant initiative and freely giving their expertise and support. In particular, I appreciate the diners who came regularly to restaurant. I learned their names; they became my friends. If I had the chance to nourish you through food, I'm honoured. I hope that if this book finds its way into your hands it will nourish you just as well.

THE ACCIDENTAL CHEF

COMMUNITY-SUPPORTED BOOK

The community I built around ZenKitchen wanted to support me in opening a restaurant, so I came up with a community-supported restaurant initiative to gather funds in advance from my diners—like a farmer does using CSA shares.

In creating this book, I called on my community for support again.

And I am so touched by the support I received. I'd like to acknowledge contributors to this "community-supported book." The following list recognizes those generous individuals who provided their financial support in creating what you hold in your hands.

Yahoo, we did it! Another labour of love out the door! Thank you so much, all.

Angela Regnier, Barb Brook, Beth Greenhorn, Bettina Vollmerhausen and Michael Peveril, Brenda Castleman, Brenda, Bob and Ziggy Conway, Carol Faulkner, Carole Saab, Chris Cornish, Clare Beckton and Ken Walper, Cris Okihiro, Deborah Rolls, Dominique Dennery, Doug Massey, Geoff Marcy, Wendy Kam Marcy and CJ Kam Marcy, Gregg Lewis, Heather Fraser, Irena Konopacki, Jennifer Howard, Jeremy Huws, Joy Flink, Karine and Nicolas Pjontek, Kathleen Burr, Katita Stark and Geoffrey Owen, Ken Rockburn, Louis Radakir, Marie-Andrée Bourgouin, Marlie Yoshiki, Michael Gazier, Michael Machida, Michael, Alice and Kate Slobodnyak, Nancy and Ron Hendrickson, Nasheen Liu and Jeffrey Ishii, Paul Jones and Jodie van Dieen, Randy Okihiro, Rell DeShaw, Shawn Murphy, Dr. Sheila A. Wong, Shirley Greenberg, Tara Peel, Tomo and Arthur Ishii, Vera Adamovich

ABOUT THE AUTHOR

 Caroline Ruriko Ishii has had a love and curiosity for food and flavours since she was a child in Toronto helping her mother prepare traditional Japanese dishes. This interest grew into a passion for the fundamentals and creativity of cooking and informed her emergence in Canada as a gifted, award-winning chef, TV personality, instructor and author.

Caroline was the creative force behind ZenKitchen—a gourmet, vegan whole foods restaurant in Ottawa that enabled her to channel the concepts formed from her childhood experiences and chef training in New York and San Francisco. These concepts—that plant-based, organic, and local, whole foods are best for our bodies and for the environment—are popular today but were trailblazing in Zen-Kitchen's early days.

Caroline's bold new take on traditional ideas quickly earned a devoted following and critical acclaim, including the silver medal at Canada's prestigious Gold Medal Plates Culinary Olympics competition in 2011 and 2012. Her popularity grew with a 13-part documentary-reality show called *The Restaurant Adventures of Caroline and Dave* that aired on the W Network, Air Canada in-flight entertainment, the Asia Food Channel, and Oprah Winfrey Network (OWN) Canada.

Caroline holds an Executive MBA from the University of Ottawa and is a graduate of the Natural Gourmet Institute for Health and Culinary Arts in New York. Following her graduation, she studied with some of the best natural food chefs in the world, interning at famous vegan and whole foods restaurants Candle 79 in New York and Millennium Restaurant in San Francisco. A long-time meditator and lover of yoga, Caroline obtained her hatha teacher training certificate from Ottawa's Prana Shanti Yoga Centre in 2013. She divides her time among living in Ottawa and Toronto and travelling the world in search of new taste memories.

The Accidental Chef is Caroline's first book.   *www.carolineishii.com*

CPSIA information can be obtained
at www.ICGtesting.com
Printed in the USA
LVOW13s0231291116

514785LV00022B/1844/P